TOP 5 ONLINE BUSINESS TACTICS (FIRE YOUR BOSS)

- With Complete Explanation
(PART – 1)

KANHA GUPTA

Copyright © 2021 **Kanha Gupta**

All rights reserved.

ISBN: 9798540377102

__DEDICATION__

To lovers of books....

I hope this book helps you to get your health to a better level, that it allows you to stir the hearts and minds of many, many people.

I would love nothing more than to see your book in the hands of people everywhere – readers walking down the street, browsers in the bookstores, vacationers at the beach, students in the classroom, secretaries at the
office, mothers at home.

That's a great challenge, and may be it's not possible to achieve. But it is certainly worth an attempt. Even several attempts.

Take your time. Do it right. Focus on your health and mind. Be happy and enjoy.

That's the best advice I can give you.

CONTENTS

- Acknowledgement   Pg 7

1) Affiliate Marketing   Pg 9
   A-To-Z!!!

2) Basics Of Blogging   Pg 55
   For Beginners

3) Thirty Most Power   Pg 76
   Words Of Marketing

4) How To Make Network   Pg 81
   Marketing Debt Free

5) How To Increase Your   Pg 101
   Sales

- About The Author   Pg 197

- Some Important   Pg 199
  Digital Products

- Thank You Note   Pg 201
  For Readers

ACKNOWLEDGEMENT

First and foremost, I would like you thank God for his never-ending grace, mercy and provision during what ended up being one of the toughest times of my life. I would also like to thank my astoundingly supportive parents, there should be no "hope" without any of you. Last but not the least, I would also like to thank my brilliant and truly outstanding friends whose visions steered this work from day one.

For those who have touched my life in any way since I've started in this book, you all know who you are, and I truly grateful for all you have done.

1.
AFFILIATE MARKETING A-TO-Z !!!

INTRODUCTION

Being withinside the associate advertising and marketing enterprise isn't always that difficult now with the net at your disposable. It is tons less difficult now in comparison to the days while humans have to utilize the phones and different mediums of statistics simply to get the ultra-modern updates at the manner their software is coming along. So with generation at hand, and assuming that the associate is operating from home, an afternoon in his or her existence could sound some thing like this... Upon waking up and after having breakfast, the laptop is grew to become on to test out new tendencies withinside the network. As some distance because the marketer is involved there is probably new matters to replace and records to preserve song on. The web page layout must be revised. The marketer is aware of that well designed web page can boom signal ups from visitors. It also can assist in the associate's conversion rates. That finished, it's time to post the associate software to directories that lists associate programs. These directories are approach to draw humans in becoming a member of your associate software. A certain manner of selling the associate software. Time to song down the income you have become out of your associates fairly and accurately. There are telephone orders and mails to song down. See if they're new customers checking the goods out. Noting down the touch statistics that is probably a possible supply withinside the future. There are plenty of sources to kind out. Ads, banners, button commercials and pattern guidelines to provide out due to the fact the marketer is aware of that that is one manner of making sure greater income. Best to live seen and handy too. The associate marketer remembered that there are inquiries to solution from the visitors. This must be finished quickly. Nothing can flip off a consumer than an unanswered email. To show that the associate is operating correctly and efficiently, inquiries could ought to be paid greater interest on. Nobody desires to be unnoticed and clients aren't continually the maximum affected person of all humans. Quick solution that must seem expert but pleasant too. In the technique of doing all of the necessities, the marketer is logged on to a talk room in which she or he interacts with different associates and the ones beneath that equal software. This is in which they are able to speak matters on the way to first-rate sell their products. There are matters to be found out and it's far a non-stop technique. Sharing recommendations and advices is a great manner of displaying support. There can be others obtainable looking to enroll in and can be enticed via way of means of the discussion this is going on. There isn't any damage in assuming what opportunities ahead. The newsletters and ezines had been up to date days ago, so it's time for the associate marketer to peer if there are a few new matters taking place in the market. This could be written approximately withinside the marketer's booklet to be disbursed to the vintage and new clients. These equal guides also are an vital device in preserving up to date with the newly delivered products. The marketer has positioned up a sale and merchandising that clients might also additionally need to understand approximately. Besides, they ought to preserve up with the cut-off date of those income written withinside the guides. It is that point to reveal a few appreciation to the ones who've helped the marketer withinside the promotions and sale boom. Nothing like citing the persons, their websites and the technique they have got finished that made the whole lot worked. Of course, this can be posted withinside the newsletters. Among the greater vital statistics which have been written already. The marketer nonetheless has time to put in writing out guidelines to the ones who need credible assitance for the goods being promoted. There is also time to publish a few feedback on the way to be a hit associate marketer on a website in which there are plenty of wannabees. Two targets finished on the equal time. The marketer receives to sell the product in addition to this system they're in. Who is aware of, someone can be willing to enroll in. Time flies.

Missed lunch however is pretty contented with the obligations finished. Bed time…. Ok, so this can now no longer be all finished in an afternoon. But then, this offers you an concept of ways an associate marketer, a committed one this is, spends the advertising and marketing day. Is that fulfillment looming withinside the distance or what?

3 Things All Affiliate Marketers Need To Survive Online

Every associate marketer is usually searching out the a success market that offers the largest paycheck. Sometimes they suppose it's miles a magic formulation this is with no trouble to be had for them. Actually, it's miles greater complex than that. It is simply top advertising and marketing practices which have been tested over years of tough paintings and dedication. There are procedures which have labored earlier than with on-line advertising and marketing and is persevering with to paintings withinside the on-line associate advertising and marketing international of today. With those pinnacle 3 advertising and marketing suggestions, you'll be capable of capable of growth your income and continue to exist withinside the associate advertising and marketing on-line.

What are those 3 procedures?

1) Using specific net pages to sell every separate product you're advertising and marketing. Do now no longer lump it all collectively simply to store a few cash on net hosting. It is pleasant to have a website specializing in every and every

product and not anything greater. Always consist of product critiques at the internet site so site visitors can have an preliminary know-how on what the product can do to individuals who buys them. Also consist of testimonials from customers who've already attempted the product. Be positive that those clients are greater than inclined to can help you use their names and pix at the web website online of the particular product you're advertising and marketing. You also can write articles highlighting the makes use of the product and consist of them at the internet site as a further web page. Make the pages appealing compelling and consist of calls to behave at the data. Each headline have to appeal to the readers to try to study greater, even touch you. Highlight your unique factors. This will assist your readers to learn what the web page is set and could need to discover greater.

2) Offer loose reviews on your readers. If viable role them at the very pinnacle aspect of your web page so it they virtually can't be missed. Try to create autoresponder messages with a purpose to be mailed to individuals who input their private data into your join up box. According to research, a sale is closed generally at the 7th touch with a prospect. Only matters can in all likelihood take place with the net web page alone: closed sale or the possibility leaving the web page and by no means go back again. By putting beneficial data into their

inboxes at positive distinctive period, you may remind them of the product they idea they need later and will discover that the sale is closed. Be positive that the content material is directed closer to particular motives to shop for the product. Do now no longer make it sound like a income pitch. Focus on crucial factors like how your product could make lifestyles and matters less difficult and greater enjoyable. Include compelling problem strains in the email. As lots as viable, keep away from the use of the word "loose" because there are nonetheless older unsolicited mail filters that dumps the ones type of contents into the junk earlier than even everybody studying them first. Convince individuals who signed up on your loose reviews that they'll be lacking some thing big in the event that they do now no longer avail of your merchandise and services.

3) Get the type of visitors this is focused on your product. Just suppose, if the individual that visited your internet site has no hobby in any way in what you're offering, they'll be amongst individuals who flow on and by no means come back. Write articles for booklet in e-zines and ereports. This manner you could discover courses this is specializing in your goal clients and what you've got positioned up may simply grasp their hobby. Try to jot down at the very least 2 articles consistent with week, with as a minimum 300-600 phrases in length. By

constantly writing and keeping those articles you could generate as many as one hundred focused readers on your web website online in a day. Always don't forget that most effective 1 out of one hundred humans are in all likelihood to shop for your product or get your services. If you could generate as lots as 1,000 focused hits on your internet site in a day, meaning you could made 10 income primarily based totally at the common statistic. The procedures given above does now no longer truly sound very tough to do, if you reflect on consideration on it. It simply calls for a touch time and an motion plan on your part.

Try to apply those suggestions for numerous associate advertising and marketing programs. You can stop keeping an excellent supply of earnings and surviving in this enterprise that now no longer all entrepreneurs can do.

Besides, think about the big paychecks you'll be receiving...

Top 3 Ways To Boost Your Affiliate Commissions Overnight

The perfect international of associate advertising does now no longer require having your won website, coping with customers, refunds, product improvement and maintenance. This is one of the simplest methods of launching into an on line enterprise and incomes extra earnings. Assuming you're already into an associate software, what could be the subsequent aspect you will need to do? Double, or maybe triple, your commissions, right? How do you do that?

Here are a few effective recommendations on a way to increase your associate software commissions overnight.

1) Know the quality software and merchandise to sell. Obviously, you could need to sell a software so as to allow you to obtain the best earnings withinside the shortest feasible time. There are numerous elements to do not forget in deciding on the sort of software.

Choose those which have a beneficiant fee structure. Have merchandise that suit in together along with your goal audience. And that has a solid song document of paying their associate effortlessly and on time. If you cannot appear to growth your investments, sell off that software and keep searching out higher ones. There are hundreds of associate applications on line which offers you the motive to be picky. You might also additionally need to pick out the quality to keep away from losing your marketing and marketing dollars. Write loose reviews or brief e-books to distribute out of your site. There is a high-quality opportunity which you are competing with different associates that are selling the equal software. If you begin writing brief file related to the product you're selling, you'll be capable of distinguish your self from the alternative associates.

In the reviews, offer a few treasured records for loose. If feasible, upload a few pointers approximately the merchandise. With e-books, you get credibility. Customers will see that during you and they'll be enticed to strive out what you're offering.

2) Collect and keep the e-mail addresses of folks who down load your loose e-books. It is a recognized truth that humans do now no longer make a buy on the primary solicitation. You

might also additionally need to ship out your message extra than six instances to make a sale.

This is the easy motive why you need to acquire the touch records of folks who downloaded your reviews and ebooks. You could make follow-ups on those contacts to remind them to make a buy from you.

Get the touch records of a prospect earlier than sending them to the vendor's website. Keep in thoughts which you are offering loose commercial for the product owners. You receives a commission simplest whilst you make a sale. If you ship possibilities without delay to the vendors, chances are they could be misplaced to you forever. But whilst you get their names, you may usually ship different advertising messages to them so that you can earn an ongoing fee instead of a one-time sale simplest. Publish a web publication or Ezine. It is usually quality to recommend a product to a person you recognize than to promote to a stranger. This is the motive in the back of publishing your very own publication. This additionally lets in you to increase a dating primarily based totally on consider together along with your subscribers.

This method is a sensitive stability among offering useful

records with a income pitch. If you still write informative editorials you'll be capable of construct a feel of reciprocity for your readers that can cause them to aid you with the aid of using shopping for your merchandise.

3) Ask for better than everyday fee from merchants. If you're already a hit with a selected promotion, you need to attempt to method the service provider and negotiate a percent fee for your income. If the service provider is smart, he or she can be able to probable provide your request rather than lose a treasured asset in you. Keep in thoughts which you are a zero risk funding for your service provider; so do now no longer be shy approximately requesting for addition for your commissions. Just attempt to be affordable approximately it. Write sturdy pay Per Click commercials. PPC seek engine is the maximum powerful approach of marketing and marketing on line. As an associate, you may make a small earnings simply with the aid of using dealing with PPC campaigns along with Google AdWords and Overture. Then you need to attempt to display them to peer which commercials are extra powerful and which of them to dispose of.

Try out those techniques and notice the distinction it is able to make for your fee tests withinside the shortest of time.

Which Affiliate Networks To Look Out When You Are Promoting?

There are many horror tales related to associate packages and networks. People have heard them again and again again, that a few are even cautious of becoming a member of one. The tales they'll have heard are the ones related to unlawful packages or pyramid schemes. Basically, this type of market does now no longer have actual, worth product.

You do now no longer need to be related to those schemes. It is obvious you need to be with a application that gives excessive great product that you'll effectively endorse. The developing quantity of people who have joined already and are succeeding immensely is evidence sufficient that there are dependable and great associate packages out there. Why take part in an associate application?

It lets in you to paintings part-time. It offers you the possibility to construct a beneficiant residual profits. And it makes you an proprietor of a small commercial enterprise. Affiliate packages have already created masses of millionaires. They are the dwelling testimony of the way tough paintings; non-stop prospecting, motivating and schooling others pay off. If ever you're identifying to sign up for one, you ought to take be aware which you are moving into some thing this is patterned to what you're able to. This may be an warranty which you are able to doing something to pop out successful. How do you select a great associate application to promote?

Here are a few suggestions you could need to appearance over earlier than selecting one:

1) A application which you like and feature hobby in. One of the best approaches of understanding if this is the type of application you want to promote is in case you are interested by shopping the product your self. If this is the case, possibilities are, there are numerous others who're also interested by the identical application and merchandise.

2) Look for a application this is of excessive great. For instance, appearance for one this is related to many specialists in that unique industry. This way, you're confident that of the same old of this system you may be becoming a member of into.

3) Join withinside the ones that provide actual and possible merchandise. How do you recognize this? Do a few preliminary research. If viable, music down a few of the contributors and clients to provide you testimonial on the credibility of this system.

4) The application this is catering to a developing goal market. This will make sure you that there may be greater and non-stop needs for your referrals. Make inquiries. There are boards and discussions you could take part in to get correct and dependable feedbacks.

5) A application with a repayment plan that will pay out a residual profits and a payout of 30% or greater could be a exquisite choice. There are a few packages imparting this type of repayment. Look carefully for one. Do now no longer waste some time with packages that do now no longer praise significantly in your efforts.

6) Be privy to the minimal quotas which you ought to satisfy or sales goal this is too tough to achieve. Some associate packages imposes pre-requirements earlier than you get your commissions. Just ensure that you're able to achieving their requirements.

7) Select one which has masses of equipment and assets which could assist you develop the commercial enterprise withinside the shortest viable time. Not all associate packages have those capacities. Make use you determine on one with masses of beneficial equipment you could use.

8) Check out if this system has a validated gadget which could permit you to test your networks and repayment. Also test in the event that they have it to be had on-line for you to test whenever and anywhere.

9) The application this is imparting sturdy incentives for contributors to renew their club every time. The associate application that presents non-stop assist and enhancements for its merchandise have the tendency to keep its contributors. These matters can guarantee the increase of your networks.

10) Be privy to the matters that contributors aren't glad approximately in a application. Like with those referred to above, you could do your checking at dialogue boards. If you realize a person in that identical application, there's ho damage asking if there are numerous downsides involved.

Have a radical and in depth information approximately the associate application and community you'll be selling on.

Knowing the type of application you have become your self into will make you count on and save you from any destiny issues you could encounter in future.

So Many Affiliate Programs! Which One I Should Choose?

Ask questions first earlier than you be part of an associate application. Do a little studies approximately the picks of application which you intend to enroll into. Get a few solutions due to the fact they may be the finding out factor of what you'll be accomplishing later on.

Will it price you whatever to enroll in? Most associate packages being offered nowadays are honestly freed from fee. So why accept the ones that fee you a few bucks earlier than joining.

When do they difficulty the fee tests? Every application is different. Some difficulty their tests as soon as a month, each quarter, etc. Select the only this is suitable in your charge time desire. Many associate packages are placing a minimal earned fee quantity that an associate need to meet or exceed so as for his or her tests to be issued.

What is the hit in keeping with sale ratio? This is the common quantity of hits to a banner or textual content hyperlink it takes to generate a sale primarily based totally on all associate statistics. This element is extraordinarily critical due to the fact this can inform you how tons site visitors you need to generate earlier than you could earn a fee from the sale.

How are referrals from an associate's web page tracked and for the way lengthy do they continue to be withinside the device? You want to be assured at the application sufficient to song the ones human beings you refer out of your web page. This is the most effective manner that you could credit score for a sale. The time period that the ones human beings live withinside the device is likewise critical. This is due to the fact a few traffic do now no longer purchase first of all however may also need to go back later to make the purchase. Know if you'll nonetheless get credit score for the sale if it's far finished a few months from a positive day.

What are the sorts of associate stats to be had? Your desire of associate application have to be able to imparting targeted stats. They have to be to be had on-line each time you make a decision to test them out. Constantly checking your character stats is critical to understand how many impressions, hits and income are already generated out of your web page. Impressions are the quantity of instances the banner or textual content hyperlink was regarded via way of means of a traveler of your web page. A hit is the only clicking at the banner or textual content links.

Does the associate application additionally pay for the hits and impressions except the commissions on income? It is critical that impressions and hits also are paid, as this can upload to the income you get from the income fee. This is in particular critical if this system you're in gives low income so that you can hit ratio.

Who is the net store? Find out whom you're doing enterprise with to understand if it's far absolutely a strong company. Know the goods they may be promoting and the common quantity they may be accomplishing. The greater you understand approximately the store imparting you the associate application, the less difficult it may be so that it will understand if that application is absolutely for you and your web page.

Is the associate a one tier or tier application? A unmarried tier application will pay you most effective for the enterprise you your self have generated. A tier application will pay you for the enterprise, plus it additionally will pay you a fee at the at the income generated via way of means of any associate you sponsor in your application.

Some -tier packages are even paying small charges on every new associate you sponsor. More like a recruitment fee. Lastly, what's the quantity of fee paid? 5% - 20% is the fee paid via way of means of maximum packages. .01% - .05% is the quantity paid for every hit. If you discover a application that still will pay for impressions, the quantity paid isn't always tons at all. As you could see from the figures, you will now recognize why the common income quantity and hit to sale ratio is critical.

These are simply a number of the questions that wanted answering first earlier than you input into an associate application. You have to be acquainted with the various critical elements that your selected application have to have earlier than incorporating them into your website. Try to invite your associate application picks those questions. These permit you to pick out the right application for you web page from some of the many to be had.

Here's How To Avoid The 3 Most Common Affiliate Mistakes

Affiliate advertising and marketing is one of the handiest and effective approaches of incomes a few cash online. This software offers all of us a chance to make a income via the Internet. Since those associate advertising and marketing packages are clean to be a part of, enforce and will pay a fee on a normal basis, extra an extra humans at the moment are inclined on this business. However, like every businesses, there are masses of pitfalls withinside the associate advertising and marketing business. Committing a number of the maximum not unusual place errors will price the entrepreneurs a huge component taken from the income they're making everyday. That is why it's far higher to keep away from them than be regretful withinside the end.

1: Choosing the incorrect associate software.

Many humans need to earn from associate advertising and marketing as speedy as possible. In their rush to be a part of one, they have a tendency to pick a bandwagon product. This is the type of merchandise that they suppose is "hot". They pick the product this is in call for with out genuinely thinking about if the product appeals to them. This isn't always a completely sensible flow obviously. Instead of leaping at the bandwagon, attempt pinnacle pick a product in that you are in reality fascinated in. For any undertaking to succeed, you have to take the time to plot and discern out your actions. Pick a product that appeals to you. Then perform a little studies approximately that product to look if they're in call for. Promoting a product you're extra obsessed with is simpler than selling one for the sake of the income only.

2: Joining too many associate packages.

Since associate packages are very clean to be a part of, you is probably tempted to be a part of multiples of associate packages to try to maximize the income you'll be getting. Besides you might imagine that there's not anything wrong and not anything to lose through being a part of many associate packages. True, that may be a first-rate manner to have more than one sources of profits. However, becoming a member of more than one packages and trying to sell all of them at the equal time will save you from targeting every one in all them. The end result? The most capacity of your associate software isn't always found out and the profits generated will now no longer precisely be as massive as you have been questioning to start with it would. The excellent manner to get fantastic end result is through becoming a member of simply one software that will pay a 40% fee at least. Then deliver it your excellent attempt through selling your merchandise enthusiastically. As quickly as you spot that it's far already making a affordable income, then perhaps you could now be a part of every other associate software. The method is to do it slowly however surely. There is genuinely no want to rush into matters, particularly with associate advertising and marketing. With the manner matters are going, the destiny is asking actual shiny and it appears associate advertising and marketing can be staying for a long term too.

3: Not shopping for the product or the usage of the service.

As an associate, you most important reason is to efficaciously and convincingly sell a service or product and to discover clients. For you to achieve this reason, you should be capable of relay to the clients that certain product and service. It is consequently hard as a way to try this whilst you your self have now no longer attempted this stuff out. Thus, you'll fail to sell and propose them convincingly. You may even fail to create a desire for your clients to avail any of what you're offering. Try the service or product for my part first earlier than you join up as an associate to look if it's far genuinely turning in what it promises. If you have achieved so, then you definitely are one of the credible and dwelling testaments aware of its benefits and disadvantages. Your clients will then sense the sincerity and truthfulness in you and this could cause them to attempt them out for themselves.

Many associate entrepreneurs makes those errors and are paying dearly for his or her actions. To now no longer fall into the equal state of affairs they were in, try and do the whole lot to keep away from making the equal errors.

Time is the key. Take the time to investigate your advertising and marketing approach and take a look at in case you are at the proper track. If achieved properly, you'll be capable of maximize your associate advertising and marketing software and earn better profits.

Using Product Recommendations To Increase Your Bottom Line

In associate marketing, there are numerous approaches wherein you may boom your profits and keep the account which you have labored so difficult for already. Most of the strategies and techniques may be discovered easily. No want to move everywhere and any further. They are to be had online, 24 hours an afternoon and seven days a week.

One of the extra vital approaches of growing associate marketing backside line and sale is thru the usage of product tips. Many entrepreneurs realize that that is one of the best approaches in selling a sure product.

If the clients or traffic agree with you sufficient, then they'll definitely agree with your tips. Be very cautious in the usage of this approach, though. If you begin selling the whole lot through advice, your credibility will certainly put on thin. This is visible specifically whilst tips are seemingly exaggerated and with out a whole lot merit.

Do now no longer be afraid to say matters which you do now no longer like approximately a given products or services. Rather than lose any factors for you, this may make your advice extra sensible and could generally tend to boom your credibility.

Furthermore, in case your traffic are virtually inquisitive about what you're providing, they'll be extra than thrilled to analyze what is right approximately the product, what isn't always so good, and the way the product will benefit them.

When you're recommending a sure product, there are a few matters to don't forget on a way to make it paintings successfully and for your advantage.

Sound just like the proper and main professional to your field. Remember this easy equation: Price resistance diminishes in direct share to agree with. If your traffic experience and trust which you are an professional to your niche, they may be extra willing to creating that purchase. On the opposite hand, in case you aren't exuding any self assurance and self-assurance in endorsing your merchandise, they'll in all likelihood experience that equal manner and could cross looking for every other products or services which is extra believable.

How do you set up this air of secrecy of expertise? By providing particular and new answers they might now no longer get everywhere else. Show evidence that what you're selling works as promised. Display outstanding testimonials and endorsements from reputable and regarded personalities, in related fields of course.

Avoid hype in any respect costs. It is higher to sound low key and confident, than to scream and are trying to find attention. Besides, you will now no longer need to sound unprofessional and feature that questioning persist with your potential clients and clients, now might you? Best to seem cool and self-assured on the equal time.

And don't forget; potentialities aren't stupid. They are certainly turning to professionals and can already realize the matters which you realize. If you back up your claims with difficult statistics and data, they might gladly placed down hundreds, or maybe lots really well worth of cash for your promotions. But in case you don't, they may be clever sufficient to try to have a take a observe your competitors and what they may be providing.

While recommending a product, it's also vital which you deliver out promotional freebies. People are already acquainted with the idea of providing freebies to selling your received merchandise. But only a few human beings do that to sell associate merchandise. Try to provide freebies that can sell or actually have a few facts approximately your merchandise or services.

Before you upload tips to you product, it's far given which you have to try to check the product and aid.

Do now no longer run the danger of selling junk merchandise and services. Just think how lengthy it took you to construct credibility and agree with amongst your traffic.

All in order to take to smash it's far one huge mistake in your part. If possible, have tips of merchandise which you have 100% self assurance in. Test the product aid earlier than you start to ensure that the human beings you're referring it to might now no longer be left excessive and dry whilst a hassle all at once arouse.

Have a observation over your associate marketplace and observes every techniques you're the using in it.

You might not be focusing at the tips that your merchandise want to have.

Your course of action is from time to time now no longer the only issue this is making your application works.

Try product advice and be amongst the ones few who have established its really well worth.

Easy Profits Using PPC In Your Affiliate Marketing Business

PPC is one of the 4 simple sorts of Search Engines. PPC is likewise one of the maximum cost-powerful methods of focused net marketing and marketing. According to Forbes magazine, PPC or Pay Per Click, bills to 8 billion bucks a 12 months and is anticipated to boom to round 10+ billion bucks via way of means of the 12 months 2019.

Let us take a short have a take a observe how PPC Search Engines work. These engines create listings and fee them primarily based totally on a bid quantity the internet site proprietor is inclined to pay for every click on from that seek engine. Advertisers bid towards every different to get hold of better rating for a particular key-word or word.

The maximum bidder for a positive key-word or word will then have the web website online ranked as number one withinside the PPC Search Engines observed via way of means of the 2d and 1/3 maximum bidder, as much as the final quantity that have positioned a bid at the equal key-word or word. Your commercials then will appear prominently at the outcomes pages primarily based totally at the greenback quantity bid you will comply with pay according to click on.

How do you are making cash via way of means of the use of PPC into your associate advertising and marketing business?

Most associate packages most effective pay whilst a sale is made or a lead brought after a vacationer has clickthrough your web website online. Your income will now no longer constantly be similar to they'll be depending on the net web website online content material and the site visitors market.

The motive why you must include PPC into your associate advertising and marketing application is that income are simpler to make than in any different form of associate application now no longer the use of PPC. This manner, you may be making income primarily based totally from the click throughs that your vacationer will make at the advertiser's website online. Unlike a few packages, you aren't paid according to sale or action.

PPC may be very innovative of your internet site. With PPC Search Engines included into your associate application, you may be capable of income from the vacationer's who aren't interested by your merchandise or offerings. The equal ones who go away your web website online and by no means comes returned.

You will now no longer most effective get commissions now no longer most effective from folks that are just looking the net and locating the goods and offerings that they desired however you may be capable of construct your online website's reputation as a precious resource. The traffic who've determined what they wanted from you web website online are probably to return back returned and evaluate what you're presenting extra closely. Then they'll ultimately come returned to look the net for different merchandise.

This form of associate application is likewise an smooth manner if you want to generate a few extra revenues. For example, whilst a vacationer on your web website online does a seek withinside the PPC Search Engine and clicks at the advertiser bided listings, the advertisers' account will then be deducted due to that click on. With this, you may be compensated 30% to 80% of the advertisers' bid quantity.

PPC isn't most effective a supply of producing smooth profits; it is able to additionally assist you sell your personal web website online. Most of the packages permit the commissions acquired to be spent for marketing and marketing with them right away and with no minimal incomes requirement. This is one of the extra powerful methods to alternate your uncooked traffic for focused surfers who has extra inclinations to buy your merchandise and offerings.

What will appear in case you whilst PPC into your associate application?

PPC generally have ready-to-use associate equipment that may be easily incorporated into your internet site. The usage equipments are seek boxes, banners, textual content hyperlinks and a few 404-mistakes pages. Most seek engines make use of custom answers and might offer you with a white-label associate application. This permits you, the use of only some traces of code, to combine remotely-hosted co-branded seek engine into your internet site.

The key blessings? Not most effective extra money generated however additionally a few extra cash at the side. Plus a life-time commissions as soon as you've got referred a few webmaster pals to the engine.

Think approximately it. Where are you able to get a lot of these blessings even as already producing a few earnings to your web website online? Knowing a number of the extra beneficial equipment you could use to your associate application isn't a waste of time. They are as a substitute a method of incomes inside an incomes.

Best realize extra approximately how you could use PPC engines like google into your associate application than miss out on a notable possibility to earn extra profits.

Using Camtasia Can Increase Your Affiliate Checks

Since there are already plenty of human beings stepping into associate marketing, it isn't any surprise that the opposition is getting stiff. The venture is to try to outdo different associates and consider methods with a view to attain this.

There also are many pointers and strategies being taught to those associate so that it will excellent plan their method for his or her application to paintings efficaciously in order that greater income can be achieved.

What higher manner to wow your possibilities and clients than to report and submit pinnacle notch, complete movement and streaming screen-captured films. Nothing like feeling your tough paintings getting paid through having your clients leaping up excitedly in first-rate anticipation to shop for your product proper there and then.

This is Camtasia in action. It is a tested fact; giving your clients some thing they are able to certainly see can explode your on-line income instantly.

You do now no longer want to have schooling and training with a view to know how this device can paintings in your associate application. Anyone can create beautiful films, from multimedia tutorials and step-through-step shows to be had on-line. The manner is like having your clients seated subsequent to you and searching at your laptop, as you display them the matters they want to peer and listen. All this accomplished step through step.

For individuals who does now no longer understand it yet, how does Camtasia works?

1) It can report your laptop pastime in a unmarried click. No want to ought to keep and assemble all of your documents due to the fact it's far recorded proper there and then.

2) Can without difficulty convert your films into internet pages. Once converted you may have your clients traveling that positive page. Videos are less difficult to recognize and absorb not like studying texts which often is a attempting element to do.

3) Upload your pages. Publish them thru blogs, RSS feed and podcasts. You might also additionally need your Camtasia films to get round and attain out to different human beings

that can be capacity clients withinside the future. Nothing like being seen in lots of websites and pages to promote it your self and get your message thru.

There are different matters you may do together along with your associate application the usage of Camtasia. You can...

- Create beautiful multimedia shows which can be tested to increase income due to the fact all of the senses are engaged. This additionally has the tendency to lessen skepticism amongst tough-to-please clients.

- Reduce refunds and different patron troubles through demonstrating visually a way to use your product and a way to do it properly. Complaints will additionally be minimized due to the fact all of the statistics and the presentation are there for the clients to simply see and listen approximately.

- Promote associate services and products the usage of visible shows. This is an powerful manner of redirecting your visitors directly in your associate internet site after they may be completed with the video. Make the maximum of the presentation through placing your web website online area in the long run and make them pass there immediately in the event that they need greater information.

- Multiple your **on-line public sale** bids exponentially **whilst you deliver** your readers a **experience** of what **you need to** offer. Based from reports, auctions that **consists of pix will increase bidding percent through** 400%. Imagine how **tons better it'll be** if it **had been films.**

- Publish **precious** informative products that **you may promote for** a miles better fee. It can be all really well worth the fee due to the overall coloured photos menu and templates that you may be the usage of.

- Minimize miscommunication **together along with your** clients. Instantly showing them what you **need they desired withinside the** first vicinity is making them **recognize surely** the essence of your **associate application.** The good element approximately multimedia is, **not anything tons** can pass wrong. It is there already.

- These are **simply a number of** the **matters you may** do with Camtasia that can be very **beneficial in** your selected associate program.

- Note that **the principle cause of the usage of Camtasia is to enhance** the income **this is generated** out of your associate application. Although it could be used for enjoyment and entertainment purposes, which isn't genuinely a valid cause why you pick to get at some stage in that trouble.

- Try to cognizance at the purpose which you have set upon your self to and acquire that with the usage of the matters that can be pretty a number of help in growing your income.

How To Become A Super Affiliate In Niche Markets

Over the beyond years, internet web website hosting has grown larger than it used to be. With greater corporations stepping into this enterprise and locating the various blessings it could provide them, the call for for internet web website hosting has in no way been higher. These appear to be the fashion of today.

Fifty one million humans have positioned up their first actual web sites on line in 2017 alone. It is predicted that through 2030, the net income enterprise will top their greenback bank. And to suppose, majority of these websites may be presenting one-of-a-kind associate packages for humans to select and take part into.

This most effective method one thing. It is less difficult now to discover the proper internet host to your application. The opportunity of great internet web website hosting corporations keeping apart themselves from the relaxation of the enterprise is anticipated. If that is done, the unprofessional and incompetent ones will suffer.

Support may be the primary attention for humans while selecting an internet host. It may be apparent that conventional marketing and marketing will emerge as much less and much less effective. Most humans could instead choose the internet host primarily based totally on matters that they see and hear. Also primarily based totally on the tips through the ones who've attempted them and feature proved to be a hit.

This is an excellent possibility for internet website hosting associates and resellers alike. There could be masses of internet website hosting and packages to select from that the issue in locating the proper one for them isn't always a problem anymore.

How does one emerge as a hit associate withinside the area of interest markets using internet web website hosting?

If you reflect on consideration on it, absolutely each person who wishes a internet site wishes an internet web website hosting enterprise to host it for them. As of now, there's certainly no main web website hosting enterprise so maximum humans select hosts primarily based totally from tips.

Usually, they get it from those which have already availed of an internet web website hosting services. With the various hosts presenting associate packages, there's the tendency to discover the only that you suppose will paintings excellent for you. Think of the product you'll be promoting. Pattern them to the web website online and spot if they are catering to the identical matters as you're.

When you've got been with one host for pretty a while and appear now no longer to be making lots regardless of all of your attempt, depart that one and appearance for every other. There isn't any use in looking to stick with one while you'll be earlier than off in every other one. Things will most effective need to get higher from there due to the fact you have already got been in worst situations.

Try this out. If you're pretty glad and glad together along with your internet host, try and see if they may be presenting an associate application you could take part on. Instead of you paying them, why now no longer make it the alternative way around; them paying you. The system may be as clean as setting a small "powered through" or "hosted through" hyperlink at the lowest of your web page and you're already in an associate enterprise.

Why select paying to your to your internet web website hosting whilst you do now no longer need to? Try to receives a commission through letting humans recognize you want your internet host.

Always recollect that once selecting an internet host, select the only that is thought for its incredible consumer support. There also are many web website hosting associate packages. Residual associate application is likewise being hosted. This is this system in which you receives a commission a percent every month for a purchaser which you refer.

This can permit you to have a steady supply of income. With perseverance, you could also be pretty a hit on this field.

There are numerous area of interest markets obtainable simply expecting the proper associate to penetrate to them and make that greenbacks dream come true. Knowing which one to get into is being assured sufficient of your potentials and the best consequences you'll be getting.

Website hosting is simply one associate marketplace you can attempt out and make a few excellent and non-stop income. Just recollect that to be a hit in your undertaking additionally method that time, **attempt** and patience is needed.

Nobody has invented the 100% ideal associate marketplace yet. But a few humans do recognize the way to make it large on this form of marketplace. It is simply knowing your form of marketplace and making the profits there.

2. BASICS OF BLOGGING FOR BEGINNERS

Blogging in 21st Century: Introduction to Online Journaling

Blogging and social networking are inextricably related withinside the feel that each contain positive functions and positive homes of 1 another. Both are geared toward developing a wide motion as a ways as multimedia interplay is concerned. Though it's miles actual that blogs can be regulated and saved very private, the primary reason of them is to attain out to a number of humans, to have a medium to voice your opinion.

Another similarity is that each those principles have existed in cyber area for nearly a decade now, however withinside the preliminary levels each had been instead different of 1 another. Only in the current instances have they been merged, and their similarity in reasons sincerely recognized. Blogging is basically finished to channel your mind out directly to a web magazine. You additionally need different humans to examine what you've got written.

This manner, you move approximately coming in contact with humans from all around the global who you might now no longer have in any other case known. Similar is the characteristic of social networking. It is a hub wherein the younger and the hearty flock. The probabilities of having an target market at such a platform are high.

The origination of the time period 'weblog' is thrilling. It turned into to begin with known as a 'weblog' which means a log or a diary or a magazine that lets you file your mind on a each day basis. In that feel it turned into instead in its primitive levels and did now no longer become an tool for propaganda immediately. This time period turned into later shortened to weblog and that is whilst free running a blog offerings like Blogger have become extraordinarily popular.

As noted earlier, running a blog these days isn't constrained to simplest preserving a magazine. It has sincerely end up a platform wherein diverse styles of humans from all walks of life, whether or not they have the equal ideologies or now no longer, conflate, and speak the subjects they suppose are critical to them.

Blogging withinside the 21st century has come to end up an critical device for advertising for individuals who want to marketplace their merchandise online, for politicians who want to promote their ideologies, and attain out, to the masses. Moreover, developing a weblog and preserving it does now no longer require a fortune. Everybody now has a private weblog and it's miles all freed from cost. Also, one does now no longer want to be a computer engineer or a photo or net fashion dressmaker which will adorn their weblog.

Unlike a internet site which operates on a exclusive domain, and for which each single template and tab desires to be designed and made from the scratch, weblog websites do now no longer want such knowledge. The running a blog provider vendors have their very own built in templates and fonts which must be selected via way of means of the bloggers as in line with their very own tastes and preferences.

Blogging is a super manner to make new buddies and are available touch with extra humans than you may do withinside the real word, from all quarters of the arena. Such numerous humans will glaringly have differing viewpoints. Therefore, this offers scope for a bargain of dialogue and debate with all factors of view being taken on board.

Blogs also can be for the only reason of creating new buddies and socializing. That is why social networking websites have picked up the clue and in those instances social networking and running a blog has, to a few extent, been combined, and nearly end up indistinguishable.

It might be thrilling to be aware that the word 'weblog' is each a noun and a verb. This leads us to the truth that running a blog in a few feel additionally allows cast off hassles of publishing.

Though your paintings will now no longer pop out in print, you already know that you may submit your paintings – your articles, pictures, videos, etc. – your self via your weblog. Therefore, it could be your very own private magazine which you want others to examine otherwise you works of artwork in phrases of the memories or articles which you write, or the films which you make. You can proportion nearly any content material with the arena at large.

It have to additionally be stated that much like you do now no longer must be an internet fashion dressmaker to create your very own weblog, you want now no longer be a expert writer, a movie maker or a photographer to submit content material in your weblog.

It is only an area on the way to take pleasure in your very own small creative interests and proportion the ones moments with others. Blogging have to consequently be exploited to its complete potential.

How Can Online Blogging Be Profitable to Ordinary Individuals?

Ranking of any internet site relies upon on some elements. It might essentially rely on the relevance of the item in keeping with the important thing phrases used; the range of instances that page has been connected and viewed, etc.

These are pretty clean to follow, and if those elements are cautiously stated and appeared into, the scores of your internet site can boom considerably.

The first step is to get your internet site connected via numerous different pages. The extra the pages are that incorporate your links, the higher rating they may obtain. The 2d aspect to be saved in thoughts is how regularly you replace the content material in your internet site.

Frequently edited and up to date websites obtain better rating in search engines like google like google and yahoo than the ones which have now no longer been checked out via way of means of the proprietors for ages. Always enhancing the content material of your internet site as an entire might not be an option.

In this situation what you could do is upload a Blog on your internet site. A Blog will characteristic as not anything however a discussion board for human beings to return back and talk the subject matters that problem your internet site too.

It will create a platform, in addition to emerge as a magazine wherein you could additionally submit updates approximately your operations and your internet site. The benefit is that the content material on such Blogs will now no longer be confined handiest to text, however pix and films may be published too.

The few clean steps as defined underneath will take you via the way to create your own weblog and what are the stuff you ought to appearance out for:

• Cost can in no way be a hassle due to the fact unfastened running a blog offerings are pretty famous all over the world. If you pick websites like Blogger or LiveJournal, you're positive to get precisely the type of platform you're looking for. They are sincerely unfastened.

• If you aren't very familiar with internet designing techniques, you want now no longer worry. Creating your weblog isn't always as complex as designing template for a internet site. These running a blog offerings offer a extensive variety of templates from which you could pick the only maximum acceptable on your tastes.

• You ought to additionally use your discretion even as running a blog. Especially in case you are incorporating your weblog inside your internet site, or developing a weblog to boom consciousness of your product, you want to hold in thoughts that that is an open discussion board that is examine via way of means of all. You do now no longer need to mention whatever which could grow to be angering your customers. Politics and faith are the 2 maximum debatable subject matters, and consequently whatever approximately the ones ought to be cautiously blogged approximately.

• Anything this is in particular reader pleasant and does now no longer anger too many human beings is taken into consideration 'safe'. If your goal is certainly to boom the rating of your site, you will ought to make certain many human beings examine it. You can do that via way of means of making your content material consumer pleasant.

- Also **hold a watch** on what **different human beings** write or say on their blogs. This can give you a **widespread concept** of what **type of responses the ones** articles **obtain, and you could get treasured pointers** from them.

Blogging has **end up taken into consideration** a noticeably **powerful advertising** tool. You can easily create **consciousness** of your product and get **customers** and **clients** to **engage** with each **different**. And **now no longer handiest clients, additionally folks who** are **exceptionally new on your product get a platform to invite** questions and **clean** their air **about** your product.

Moreover, it **additionally will increase** your **internet site scores** can **boom due to the fact** the **weblog is continuously** being updates, commented on, and discussions are **continually** going on. Because of its sheer activity, the **scores** improve, **developing extra consciousness** of the product.

The following are the **suggestions primarily based totally** on which **you could weblog approximately** your product:

- Never make the **weblog submit** too **lengthy** uselessly. It ought to be properly written. Long posts **generally tend** to get dreary and they're now no longer 'catchy' sufficient for human beings to take a seat down and go via them.

- Update regularly. Since you don't want to write down lengthy posts, that isn't always much effort. Ideally, weblog 3-7 instances a week.

- Be enjoyable wherein required, anyone can do with a few mild hearted humor, with out being derogatory.

- You want now no longer stick handiest to text. Video and photos running a blog are fat catching on and are thrilling methods to proportion your thoughts, and make your films and pix properly known.

- Be yourself. Do not to ape, imitate or replica a person else's content material.

How to Start Your Own Blog in Less than 15 Minutes

Creating a weblog is not anything which you want to be afraid of. There isn't any complicated planning required either. However, there are some matters you'll want to determine. Since those running a blog carrier carriers provide you with loads of desire in phrases of template and colour themes, could be require to take the ones choices yourself.

The following is a short manual of what to assume over earlier than developing your weblog:

• **Theme:** Determine what you'll be writing approximately or the character of the content material which you could be sharing together along with your readers. This relies upon especially in your interest. Topics running a blog to the sector of politics, poetry, arts, cutting-edge affairs, or nearly something below the solar may be chosen. You can keep on with one subject or you can select to put in writing approximately anything worries you on a day after day basis. Since it is your very personal net journal, you could make it as bendy as viable in all aspects.

- **Blogging Provider:** Next you want to determine upon which running a blog carrier issuer you would love to use. This relies upon at the form of opinions which you get approximately them from pals and friends, or some thing approximately them which you may also have examine online. Otherwise, you could usually strive out some thing and discover out if you want it. You can strive out this sort of famous websites: Blogger.com, WordPress.com, Typepad, Blogagotchi.com, Livejournal.com, JournalHome.com, TheDiary.org, Mindsay.com, Blog.com, Diaryland.com, Blogdrive.com, or Xanga.com.

- **Templates:** A huge variety of templates could be made to be had on any running a blog carrier you make a decision to begin you weblog. Select the only you maximum choose or like.

- **Freebies:** The gain with those running a blog carrier carriers is they make your running a blog revel in as dynamic and interactive as viable. They enable you to put in upload-on capabilities that consist of button, pictures, weblog chalks, imoods, tagboards including myshoutbox.com, visitor maps, guestbooks, remark boxes for readers' mind and views, etc.

- **Additional Features:** These thrilling ones might not be free. By paying a price you could avail of them.

• **Nature of Blog:** You should decide who have to examine your weblog-whether or not you need it to be examine most effective through a pick circle, or should it's open to all. This will depend on the content material, especially.

• **Layout:** Again, there could be a huge variety to select from in phrases of format and colour schemes.

• **Content:** You should choose out up a particular subject and write approximately it consistently, or simply determine on any random subject matter as and whilst it pursuits you. You should strive setting up content material for some time and spot the form of reaction you get, and modify or regulate it accordingly.

• **Blogging Circle:** Blogging is a wonderful manner to are available in contact with humans from throughout the globe. You can surf and go to different humans's blogs. Do now no longer unsolicited mail in their remark section, however write a true remark when you have some thing to say approximately a specific post.

• **Skins:** You can customize your weblog as a good deal as you need. Using software program like Photoshop you could create your personal skins and make your weblog appealing in addition to make it mirror you personal personality.

• **Publish:** Finally whilst you are executed deciding on the placing and preferences, deciding on a content material to position up, you want to submit the content material. Do now no longer, however, neglect about to ship the hyperlink on your weblog on your pals and friends in order that they may also come go to you.

Once you've got began out your weblog, you'll have observed that it rarely takes fifteen mins to do so. Maintain the weblog is even easier. Here are some recommendations that could help you efficiently preserve your weblog going:

• **Update:** Update regularly in any other case traffic may also prevent coming on your weblog. It will additionally provide you with greater self assurance to churn out greater nicely worded posts withinside the future.

• **Personalize:** Even though you are probably discussing about well known and universal themes, upload your personal private contact to make matters lighter and thrilling.

• **Theme:** If you've got a subject weblog you could Google for different blogs of a comparable kind and construct you network.

- **Spelling and Grammar:** Make certain you evidence examine your posts. Spelling and grammatical mistakes may be a primary put-off for lots readers.

- **Advertisements:** You should play host to websites like Google AdSense and earn sales through putting their hyperlinks in your weblog.

Writing Content and Getting Constant Traffic to Your Blog

Blogging has simply revolutionized the manner one studies the virtual age. There is, it seems, no restrict to what you will do with the assist of blogs. Even the smallest element of your each day private existence like recording magazine entries has been given a wholly new dimension.

Going on from there, there is lots of scope of selecting up exciting debates and discussions via blogs. You may even begin a number of those discussions your self. Moreover, there may be not anything as exciting and appealing than that reality that you could even earn a few cash at the same time as running a blog.

This is, via way of means of far, the maximum route breaking innovation that has entered the weblog sphere. The necessities for this are very low. You want now no longer be a scientist who posts revolutionary information about his contemporary experiment.

If you weblog nicely, this is to say, in case you weblog nicely sufficient for human beings to return back study it, you earn suitable possibilities of creating short cash, via way of means of simply going approximately your each day interest of posting blogs!

Here are a number of the matters you could do to make certain that your running a blog sports get rewarded via way of means of greater than simply remarks and praises:

You should get your self registered with a seek engine. But maintain in thoughts which you should do it most effective in case you are assured sufficient that your weblog receives suitable visitors. That manner, the better the rating your weblog achieves, the greater you get paid.

While writing your blogs you furthermore may want to maintain in thoughts some matters. This isn't always most effective to make certain which you get a consistent visitors, however additionally for the reality that your weblog readership can boom in order that the rating of your weblog with search engine moves better.

Here are some guidelines that ought to see you via this:

- **Reader Friendly Content:** At all expenses maintain your content material – articles, poems, photographs, videos – reader pleasant, this is to say, it ought to maintain greater and greater readers interested. Your reader should be on the middle of you submit in a manner that your reader should sense that he's gaining some thing out of analyzing your submit. This is the primary rule in marketing.

• **Worthwhile:** Never permit the reader sense that he has been tricked into analyzing your submit or clicking in your weblog hyperlink. You are thwarting all of your long time possibilities of that reader coming again in your weblog, wherein case your weblog ratings over the long time are in a dicey position.

• **Check for mistakes:** Making grammatical and spelling mistakes may be a primary positioned off for plenty readers. They won't go to your weblog once more certainly due to the fact the mistakes which you make are too high. Always evidence study your weblog. A small typo right here and there may be understood, however make certain you don't make any foremost mistakes.

• **KISS:** Or, Keep It Short and Simple. This is the thumb rule you should comply with at all factor. Long winding posts have a tendency to get boring. And it could comprise not anything this is exciting to the reader. Also no person has the time sufficient to your weblog, no count number how nicely you write. In reality, your weblog could be an awful lot greater favored in case you positioned your mind certainly and shortly.

- **Interesting:** Make positive which you maintain your reader's interest via way of means of making your posts snazzy. They should now no longer be written in a tone this is tiring to study. Write short sentences and maintain then crisp and precise. Always hit the factor right now in the path of your article.

- **Link:** Keep linking the blogs you study to yours as a way to construct a community those human beings could be in flip advocated to hyperlink you. Remember, linking will increase ratings.

- **Keywords:** Using the key phrases of your posts often will increase the seek capacity of that precise article of yours which in flip leads greater human beings to go to your weblog.

- **Clear Thoughts:** Make positive you positioned your notion sincerely earlier than the readers so that it does now no longer turn out to be tedious for them to study.

- **Colloquialism:** You can write in a pleasant tone. Avoid the use of too many slang words, however otherwise, in case your submit needs it, you could be casual.

- **Post Title:** A catchy submit name or headline is 1/2 of your commercial enterprise solved. It can glue a reader in your submit nearly right now. However, do now no longer positioned deceptive submit titles, or you'll lose creditability.

So, be steady together along with your weblog content material and watch visitors flowing in your weblog!

3.
THIRTY MOST POWER WORDS OF MARKETING

- **You** – Write as though you're talking to the purchaser and approximately about the product, no longer about yourself.

- **Because** – Give clients a purpose why they want to take some action.

- **Free** – "Because" all of us like loose things, isn't?

- **Value** – This implies clients have become some thing versus dropping some thing (i.e. cash while you say "cost" or "price").

- **Guaranteed** – Give clients a assure to decrease danger notion, so that they sense they've the whole lot to benefit and not anything to lose.

- **Amazing** – Customers will reply to some thing that is incredible.

- **Easy** – Make it easy for clients to take the following step withinside the buying process, and allow them to recognize how plenty simpler existence will be together along with your services or products.

- **Discover** – This implies there may be some thing new and unknown to the purchaser, some thing that has superb advantages and offers them a benefits.

- **Act now** – Motivate a right away reaction with a limited-time provide.

- **Everything included/the whole lot you want** – This establishes that your services or products is all of your clients may have to shop for in order to reap their goal.

- **Never** – Point out a "bad benefit," such as "by no means worry again" or "by no means overpay again."

- **New** – Your services or products is the slicing area in your industry.

- **Save** – The maximum effective phrase to exhibit financial savings, or maybe time savings.

- **Proven** – Remind clients that your product, carrier or enterprise is tried-and-true.

- **Safe and effective** – "Proven" to decrease danger notion for fitness and financial loss.

- **Powerful** – Let clients recognize that your enterprise, services or products is robust.

- **Real results/assured results** – Your clients need results, after all.

- **Secret** – Not everybody succeeds, and there are secrets and techniques to success. Let clients recognize you may screen the ones secrets and techniques.

- **The** – This implies your answer is the "end-all-be-all." Consider the difference: "Three Solutions for Marketing Success" and "The three Solutions for Marketing Success."

- **Instant** – Instant get admission to or downloads are extra attractive than waiting.

- **How to** – Start off with an answer so clients study the relaxation of your copy.

- **Elite** – Your clients are most of the high-quality withinside the world. Invite beginners to sign up for a surprisingly appropriate club.

- **Premium** – Premium allows denote excessive quality.

- **Caused by** – If your advertising literature builds a case in your product, transitional terms such as "brought on by," "therefore," and "thus" can assist enhance the common sense of a purchase.

- **More** – Do you provide extra than your competitors? Let your clients recognize, due to the fact they need the high-quality deal, after all.

- **Bargain** – Because clients need a extremely good deal, remember?

- **No obligation** – Create a win-win state of affairs in your clients.

- **100% cash-return assure** – Again, no danger.

- **Huge** – A massive cut price or super provide is tough to resist.

- **Wealth** – If you're promoting services and products associated to cash, wealth is a appropriate phrase for clients

4.
HOW TO MAKE NETWORK MARKETING DEBT FREE

A Business Just Like Any Other

What is the **reason of beginning a enterprise?** To make earnings.

Most **agencies** spend **extra money** than they make that's why they **cross stomach** up.

So why **must community advertising and marketing** be any different?

The **usual mindset** is that **community advertising and marketing** is a **enterprise** that appreciates in value over time. In **different** words, if I actually have a collection of **a hundred to 1,000 human beings beneath** me **shopping for** the product and recruiting **greater**, I'd be getting richer and richer! But **all of us recognize** that.

It **isn't the pot of gold on the give up** of the rainbow. It's SURVIVING the **primary** 6 months to 2 years! It is **casual** that maximum community entrepreneurs in a brand new enterprise normally undergo a 6 months trial and **blunders** period, therefore, it's miles essential to make certain that in the ones 6 training months, you manipulate your coins accurately so that you can research and make cash on the same time.

Just like in ordinary enterprise, maximum of them fail inside their first 2 years of operation and warfare to make earnings although they do survive. The key to survival is CASH FLOW.

In different words, it may be summed up on this equation: **Cash today, downline tomorrow**.

People in community advertising and marketing normally run out of coins waft generally after three months and they stop due to the fact they spend greater as they build. But through breaking whilst rapid as possible, it offers exceptional intellectual electricity to the distributor and she is less probably to drop out.

First, we should recognize the mind-set that is the maximum essential place to begin in getting through the primary three months.

The Mindset of a Business Builder

(Don't continue any in addition on this book till you ingrain those into your brain!)

- It takes TIME to construct a hit enterprise. If you are making ANY cash in the first few months (although it's miles only a few dollars) it's PERFECTLY ALRIGHT.

- It is MY BUSINESS. Not my upline's enterprise or my downline's enterprise. Everything relies upon on ME setting attempt to succeed.

- Invest in TOOLS that brings in revenue (lead generators, viral e-books, generic information, etc). Don't purchase books and tapes only for the sake of purchasing them.

- Don't use your personal cash if possible. Most a hit businessmen use different humans's cash (borrowed cash both from spouse and children or economic institutions) to construct their enterprise. Remember that money go with the drift is greater vital than revenue.

- Don't blow all of your cash on marketing and marketing that doesn't carry in coins go with the drift as well. Direct reaction marketing and marketing is one of the best ways.

- A clever businessman doesn't unfold himself out too much. Build the LOCAL marketplace first. Never assignment outstation until you've got a constant income. If you can't even contend with yourself, how are you going to contend with your downline far from you?

- Focus on fixing different humans's issues. Don't recruit humans only for the sake of recruiting them. Try and apprehend what issues they're going through first.

- Enjoying the journey! People who love their task usually outperform folks who do it grudgingly. If your prospect sees you doing all of your enterprise so grudgingly, will they be part of you?

Typical MLM cash flow

Only for **instance functions** only.

Typical Mean American worker's annual salary:

Hour	$19.13
Day	$153.04
Month	$3,316.25
Year	$39,795

Expenses:

Joining Fee	$50 - $5,000
Auto-ship	$5 - $500
Fuel	$300
Training Expenditure	$200 - $500
Meetings and Rallies	$50 - $8,000
Telephone Bill	$100 - $500
Leads	$200 - $500
Extras	$200 - $500

Depending at the community advertising and marketing company, do you notice how usual it's miles for an common builder to spend someplace between $1,000 to $16,000 as a STARTING INVESTMENT? You can estimate how tons you need to make in the end then only will you spoil even. But allow us to see how we will decrease those overheads to generate greater coins flow.

What is Your Profit Margin?

One of the important thing techniques to generate greater coins waft is referring to your COMPENSATION PLAN.

Different plans might also additionally range from corporation to corporation. Some corporations might also additionally boast of their excessive payout. They will say some thing like this:

Our corporation is the nice due to the fact we pay out seventy five% of our fee to all of the distributors! It is like pronouncing for every dollar one hundred sale; dollar seventy-five is paid returned to our people. You will in no way fail with this corporation!

I urge you to make sensible monetary selections and NOT emotional selections due to the fact responding to emotional attraction can motive plenty of heartaches withinside the future.

I can't cowl all of the mechanics on plans, however it's miles higher to consult the book collection called Show me The

Plan! But for the motive of this topic, I will listing down a few principles (advertising plan related) to follow.

• Don't examine the full payout of the corporation; examine the primary 2 ranges of payout: How an awful lot you get for recruiting someone, and what kind of you get if THEY recruit someone. It isn't any factor dreaming how an awful lot you're making as a 'Rainbow Diamond Leader' in case you can't even be successful on the decrease ranges.

• Examine how an awful lot you need to spend to RECRUIT someone. Some corporations require you to both pay for his or her schooling application first, or require you to accompany them into the schooling session (and you need to pay your personal way).

• If you've got little coins waft however desire to enroll in a corporation that calls for a large stock funding however excessive income margin, make certain the ones merchandise can be used to SPONSOR your downline so that you can get well as an awful lot coins as possible.

• Can you manage to pay for the auto-ship?

What About Downline: An Asset or a Liability?

What is the earnings you're waiting for out of your commercial enterprise? Do you recognize which you have to make investments money and time to your downlines? Yes, it's miles real which you make cash when your downline joins you or makes a sale, however maximum of the time, to construct a protracted term commercial enterprise; you need to make investments closely of their education.

Network Marketing is a commercial enterprise of duplication and despite the fact that many human beings can pay the rate to construct their community, you ought to be very selective of whom you spend it slow with. You can't viable be the whole thing to everybody and also you ought to pick who're the human beings that you're going locations with!

It makes feel due to the fact they time you spend with one manner time in which you could both be growing any other or recruiting a brand new distributor. Furthermore, you need to force out of your private home to peer them or accompany them in schooling and counseling sessions.

Are you **organized** to pay the **rate** for 'this guy'?

Most of the time many **human beings cease community advertising isn't always due to the fact** they **couldn't recruit, however due to the fact** they spend an excessive amount of time with a recruit **wondering they could evolve** a duck into an eagle. You quack with **geese however leap** with eagles, if I am now no longer **mistaken. So** in case you **spend** an excessive amount of time with a duck that quacks **lots however** doesn't do **some thing else, you haven't any preference however to depart** him **in the back of in case you want** to **leap** with the eagles (otherwise you **could be** like the 'duck' as well).

The key **factor** to **bear in mind** is this:

If you're doing 99% of the paintings to your community at the same time as the relaxation is doing 1%: START FINDING NEW DOWNLINES, They will spend much less of your cash (and free up it slow to make more).

In the **following couple of** chapters, I will **display you ways through erasing a number of** the **fees** on Network Marketing, you and **all of your** downlines can **keep money and time** (so your downlines will **now no longer cease without difficulty** because of loss of coins waft and your commercial enterprise will survive **higher** in **the sooner** stages).

Front-End: Consistent Stream of Income

A lot of community entrepreneurs make a completely large mistake of their business. They don't develop a couple of streams of earning and that they depend simplest on making a living via one source that is the corporation they're in. What do I mean?

Let's say I am with XYZ Company. I experience that XYZ Company has the first-class recognition in the international, the first-class product, the first-class advertising and marketing plan, has helped tens of thousands and thousands of humans withinside the international with the product and opportunity (you get the idea). Because I am so engrossed with my corporation, I refuse to interact different streams of profits like shopping for or endorsing the alternative merchandise of different businesses. Some even move as some distance as to study simplest inside their personal community advertising and marketing network simplest.

Let me emphasize as soon as again, **Network Marketing is a BUSINESS.** You have to be receptive to new thoughts and continuously study (even from different community advertising and marketing businesses!)

As a businessman, you have to be savvy sufficient to conform to conditions and do WHATEVER IT TAKES (so long as it's miles ethical) to get the activity done.

This way that your wondering have to be bendy sufficient to pop out with thoughts that accomplish the subsequent steps:

- Generate infinite leads so that you could have a big call list
- Create regular Cash Flow to live alive in Network Marketing
- Recruit downline and teach them to execute a majority of these steps

How can we accomplish the subsequent steps?

(1) Adopt the attitude of abundance. Help different humans to get what they need and subsequent time, they'll honestly assist you get what you need. Go all out to assist others and don't be stingy or calculative.

(2) Focus on growing a patron base via way of means of servicing them via the product. Focus on fixing their issues with the product. Even when you have to spend time to

construct the rapport with the patron, recall that after the patron sees exceptional outcomes out of your product, they'll promote for you willingly. A glad patron's testimonial may be very powerful. Repeat income from the glad patron (and the humans round them) will make certain a regular coins waft.

(3) BARTER TRADE your corporation's product with networkers from OTHER businesses! If I even have masses of inventory from my corporation (both via purchasing in bulk or from my auto-ship), possibilities are, there are networkers in different businesses are greater than inclined to alternate with you considering the fact that they have got masses of inventory also. With new varieties of inventory for your hand, you're capable of faucet into different markets and construct rapport with them so that you can introduce them in your important opportunity. (If my corporation simplest sells cosmetics and no dietary supplements, I can discover a networker withinside the complement like and change merchandise to faucet the complement market.)

(4) Join associate applications on line that generate coins waft in case you are Internet savvy. Find associate applications that can help you take part for a completely low price or unfastened. Remember the precept which you need to generate coins waft and assist different humans clear up their

issues. This places you in a role to as soon as again, construct rapport together along with your capacity possibilities and generates you leads. Viral advertising and marketing the use of e-books or electronic mail is a great manner to divert visitors in your associate applications and that they price very little.

(5) Give away unfastened facts on community advertising and marketing (there are plenty of unfastened or low price e-books or viral advertising and marketing equipment across the net) or write unfastened articles on your merchandise and put up them in your friends, buddies or families. For example: If you're withinside the fitness industry, write (or interview an expert) an editorial about preferred fitness problems or fitness dietary supplements as a way to provide your capacity possibilities attention on their fitness and while they're curious they'll ask you for greater facts. You can percentage your product with them afterwards.

Developing Your Own Turn-Key System

Network Marketing is a enterprise for your-self, no longer way of your-self.

Although there no difficult and rapid rule or any magic system that I can recommend, because any gadget making a decision to create will range from enterprise to enterprise, you could develop your personal turn-key gadget inside your organization.

What this indicates is that this type of gadget is designed with the group in thoughts wherein you and all of your downline all FOLLOW THE SAME SYSTEM as a popular outline. Everybody desires to move withinside the equal course as a group and a unmarried minded cognizance on achieving the group goal is vital.

Here are a few hints I can recommend to you:

- Hold nearby education periods except the enterprise's education periods on line or offline with all of your group contributors

- Educate all of the group contributors approximately right coins go with the drift hints while building the enterprise. Give every body unfastened cloth to review.

- Everyone determine how a lot attempt need to be positioned in, for example, a weekly or month-to-month goal quantity to achieve.

- Training periods on a way to use on line structures that generate leads or using associate websites (in case your enterprise sponsors one). You may also even paintings collectively to create your personal group website.

- Buddy gadget to reduce prospecting costs (like using to the meetings collectively or prospecting collectively)

- Brainstorming thoughts on different approaches to keep costs (for example: becoming a member of a phone plan collectively as noted above).

The key factor to take into account is that this:

Everyone need to cognizance on following the equal gadget

to your group!

It is **vital** for duplication. Can you **consider a hundred human beings** all **stepping into** their **personal course?** It smells like a recipe for disaster.

The **closing purpose** is to **teach** a group of independent, **coins** producing downlines who are MAKING MONEY and **supporting** their downlines to do the **equal.**

Because **ultimately** of the day, how **true** your turn-key **gadget seems displays** heavily on you **via** the **fulfillment** of your downlines.

What is the **factor** of sponsoring 10-20 **human beings, and the subsequent** week **there's handiest** 1 or 2 left **withinside the enterprise?** If attrition **could be very excessive to your network,** it's miles even **greater with the intention to create a gadget on your downline.**

Summary and Conclusion

Let me make a precis of all of the ideas on this topic.

(1) Cash float is extra vital than revenue

(2) Cash these days way extra leads, extra posture, extra training and hence: MORE DOWNLINE

(3) Expenses may be minimized. Spend simplest on what you actually need for your business

(4) Make certain your downline succeed. When you assist them make money, they will assist YOU make money!

The adventure to fulfillment can be lengthy and hard, however usually bear in mind that it isn't WHEN you end the community advertising and marketing race, it's far the way you get there through supporting others along the way, be a part of you on the end line.

Never end the community advertising and marketing race alone without your downline.

5.
HOW TO INCREASE YOUR SALES

Introduction

Let me ask you a question. The remaining time you released your personal product to sell online, or maybe offline, how did you return back to a end approximately what fee you had been going to be promoting at?

At a guess, I'd in all likelihood say you checked out the opposition to look what they had been charging. While this is a superb start, it's some distance from the complete picture, and you're fumbling withinside the darkish in case you searching at opposition is the handiest component you're taking into account.

Did you realize you may double your income quantity through doubling your fee? I've executed it myself, and I'll display you how.

Did you furthermore may recognize that 99% of the goods I see being bought are too cheap. So a good deal so, that they're placing clients off rather than attracting them (that's no doubt what they suppose they're doing).

Let's dispel a few pricing myths and dig proper right all the way down to the actual information to make sure you get the maximum coins to your pocket the subsequent time you release one in all your products.

1. Overview on Pricing

- To introduce the **principles** of fluid pricing strategies, and **to** reveal which you have many **extra** avenues to **discover** than it looks like in the beginning glance.

- To **solution** a number of your **questions** on the way you have to fee your product for **most earnings** taking the **variety** of **income** to **fee** ratio's into account.

- To show the **impact** of pricing too low, **in which** many human beings fee their merchandise with out first searching on the all critical larger picture.

- To **display** you why many **human beings** are **beneath** pricing their **merchandise** in a huge manner, and the way you could keep away from this pitfall.

- To display you that the fee you pick in your product isn't always sincerely approximately charging much less than the competition, in truth with the aid of using charging extra, you could be making even extra income.

- To provide you with extra pricing alternatives in your foremost product, and display you how you could considerably boom your income sincerely via giving your customers alternatives.

- To show the best and handiest manner of going approximately introducing trial durations in your merchandise, and why many get this wrong.

- To display you powerful strategies of experimenting together along with your fee over time without disturbing the individuals who offered from you formerly at a better fee.

Pricing Strategies - Getting Started

There are a few matters that I need to speak to you approximately associated with pricing earlier than you head off, create a income system, placed up a internet site and stuff a rate in your product.

The goal of this record is to offer a few perception into the flexibility you've got as an on line marketer together along with your very own merchandise. The trouble is, maximum human beings simply seem to whack a rate on their merchandise with little time spent considering it, why they have got priced it like that, and what elements are going to make a contribution to whether or not it is a a success decision. Sound complex and quite a few work? Well, allow me to inform you it is not.

But I suppose it is clearly essential that I display you simply how a great deal freedom to test you've got almost about pricing, and what impact getting it incorrect can have in some of ways, so earlier than you placed a rate in your product and release it to the world, make the effort out, have a read, choose up the factors and take them into consideration the use of them as form of a checklist.

The Bigger Picture

Now understand, there may be a far larger image to this than maximum human beings realize. A lot of the time expenses are placed there, simply due to the fact they may be and likely fitted loosely round opposition and different services and products supplying similar things, however, it is now no longer pretty much planting a variety of and a greenback signal at the back of it. All thru this method you must be asking your self masses of why questions. Some of the time, human beings inquire from me why the heck I pass so intensive into topics and communicate approximately why they happen. They simply need to realize a way to make an entire load of coins actual quick.

Well, I say to them I can let you know a way to do stuff, however if the scenario changes, and you did not realize why it labored withinside the first place, then you'll have to come proper lower back to me again, hand me some other 5 hundred greenbacks simply to find out a way to do the equal factor in a one of a kind manner. However, if I let you know how things work, you could take a few severe know-how and understanding away with you, and you've got the electricity to evolve to the quick paced converting global of commercial enterprise online or offline. If you can not adapt, you are dead. Or your commercial enterprise is anyway.

Like I say, there may be pretty plenty to this, and plenty of factors that we are going to communicate approximately, and there may be going to be a load of questions which are going to pop into your head. Does opposition count in one of these large market with reference to pricing? Should I be cheaper? Should I be extra expensive? How do I realize while to be which and why? Should I supply unique gives to precise organizations of human beings? Who? Why? Should I provide one of a kind variations of my product at one of a kind expenses? How do I do that, and the way do I realize if I'm doing proper?

There's a shed load of solutions approximately the above and lots extra that I'm going to provide you with in a moment. But all of the manner thru this I need you to maintain in thoughts the flexibility you've got as a web marketer together along with your pricing. Get this proper, and it should without problems imply double the earnings for you. Get it wrong, and it is probable you'll have hassle promoting some thing at all.

Pricing with Regard to Competition

So, with the formalities and generalizations out of the way, we could have a take a observe how you have to rate your merchandise in regards to competition. The purpose I need to talk approximately this first, is easy. When you are looking at pricing, the first actual thing you are in all likelihood to do is say, hey, so what's everybody else charging for similar merchandise? And you can cross from there.

Now there may be not anything incorrect with doing this at all, however there may be extra to assume approximately, and lots extra inquiries to ask than a easy can I beat what this man is charging for his carriers?

Your rate does not ought to beat everybody else's accessible which will get income. This is something that I discovered a long term ago, and you can don't forget me speaking approximately sincerely growing my income with the aid of using setting the rate of the monthly club up, and imparting an alternative that become sincerely ten instances extra money up front, which accelerated income even further.

You actually need to be aware about what different humans are charging for his or her merchandise, however that does not with the aid of using any approach sign that you need to exit there and beat them. Imagine you've got simply began out up an advert monitoring and autoresponder script site it's so detailed, and so expert that it smacks the pants off the competition. But see the alternative websites imparting the identical carrier are hanging round at the 10 greenback in keeping with month mark. Does this imply that you need to cross and beat them and feature a decrease rate for every person to have a take a observe you?

Nope, now no longer at all. What you've got to your fingers is a top rate product, and also you should not be concerned to promote it at a top rate.

Rule 1: Premium Products Sell at Premium Prices

So, here's rule variety one. If you've got a extremely good top class product, do not be afraid to bump the rate up. You do now no longer via way of means of any way need to beat a competitor's rate to be competitive, in fact, via way of means of placing your rate up, it is pretty viable that you'll outsell your inexpensive competition. Why? Because a better rate screams quality. Don't, for one moment, accept as true with you need to have the great rate to make any income. That's simply now no longer true, you simply need to have the great income system, and of route a top class product in case you simply ever need all people to shop for from you again.

Rule 2: Wowing Through A Price Is a Bad Move

The reality is, in case your fee is simply too low, human beings examine you and surprise why the heck you are charging that tiny amount. If your emblem spanking new piece of advanced generation software program is definitely as proper as you are saying it is, why does it most effective price ten dollars? So there we've rule range two. Never fee your self so low that you suppose human beings will appearance and suppose wow that's a nice sounding product, appearance how little it costs! That's now no longer what they may be announcing at all. They're announcing, "Wow, examine how little that costs. There cannot be that a whole lot to it."

So in effect, all you are doing right here is including even extra price on your product via a better fee. It is probably the identical product, however I inform you now, it is a whole lot much more likely to promote extra copies at a fee that a person may examine and suppose that it is reasonable, or common than some thing a person may examine and fall off their chair at how reasonably-priced you are.

Don't Be Afraid

Too many humans are afraid to take the bounce and rate their merchandise as they agree with they are worth. Too many humans study opposition and suppose they have to price much less in any other case nobody goes to shop for their stuff, or they will make much less cash out of it. This is sincerely now no longer true. Don't undervalue yourself only for the sake of being cheaper. If you've got a higher product, you placed a better rate tag on it. The experimentation and gambling round to locate the proper aggregate of offers, deals, follow-up and pricing alternatives can come later.

I may want to display you such a lot of merchandise which are obtainable proper now, in opposition with every different, however one is charging a heck of lots greater than the different. How approximately this guide, for one? Here's us charging you one thousand bucks for the whole set of manuals, however there are masses of different courses obtainable that price ten bucks. Will the fine of each of them be the same? Looking on the rate alone, from a customer's factor of view, I distinctly doubt it.

Time is Changing - Business Needs To Adapt

How approximately the today's buy you made in your house, whether or not it turned into a whole paintings surface, a brand new storage door, a toaster, a dinner table, something it turned into. I bet in case you reflect on it, you may see that instances have changed. A long term ago, even earlier than I turned into born, human beings desired matters that worked. They have been simply OK. But in recent times that is now no longer enough. It's were given to be the best, the fastest, the nicest, the simplest to use. There's a actual marketplace for top rate merchandise emerging. Make sure you do not location yours withinside the good deal bin if it is supposed as top rate product, now no longer a good deal basement product.

Increase Sales by Presenting Choices

OK sufficient of that for now. I need to speak approximately some thing else it's not often done, mainly withinside the global of on line advertising and information merchandise, and that is providing specific rate plans from the phrase go. Sure humans may alternate their rate, put it up and right all the way down to experiment, placed on gives and so on, however it's now no longer doing much in case your authentic plan is not nicely idea out.

Even with the only of unmarried sale information merchandise along with this, you are presented with options. The more, the higher to be honest. Whether you are a excessive price tag item providing smaller chunks to be paid at prolonged periods, or a low priced club webpage that does the opposite, and gives a lump sum that offers access for 3 months, six months or maybe a year.

Remember, the income system is all approximately answering the customer's questions, and squashing their fears or any issues they'll give you of their minds for now no longer shopping for your product. It's no properly you promoting a person on some thing and then they discover they do not have the price alternative they need. Make certain you upload multiples of these. It's simple, if there may be everyone accessible with a internet site that most effective gives one price alternative, they are dropping income. Don't permit this be you.

Rewards for Customers Is Equal To More Cash in your Pocket

Rule five, and one of the maximum critical. Never ever, regardless of what you do, forget about the human beings which have bought from you before. It's now no longer tough to return back up with approaches to praise them. Right now, I'm setting collectively an ID variety system for myself that permits preceding clients to return back alongside and purchase my stuff at a discounted rate.

These human beings are the maximum critical of all. You've already were given them for your lists, they have already offered your stuff, because of this that they may be inclined to spend money, and of path they accept as true with you, and they may be severe approximately looking greater information, or the goods and offerings you offer. Remember this, due to the fact in case you forget you may move broke. It's as easy as that. You need to preserve the clients that are shopping for from you happy, and also you need to live in contact with them. If you do not move from your manner to thrill them, you may must exit and spend wads greater on locating new clients. Look after them, due to the fact they may be with you for a long time to return back and could shape the bottom of a success enterprise from the phrase move.

Trials & Lead Generation

Rule range six: Avoid unfastened trials except you are aiming for lead generation. The trouble with unfastened trials is that you will appeal to all styles of freebie seekers, and simply like I do not need everyone right here that does not need to make a a success commercial enterprise of themselves, I'm certain you do not need humans losing it slow either, taking up treasured assets and simply choosing some thing up as it's of zero cost.

As I found out with my huge test webpage returned withinside the day, it is higher to fee a small quantity for a brief trial, say one to 3 bucks for the primary week definitely to kind the ones humans out which can be coming to you simply due to the fact they can, and the ones which can be coming to you due to the fact they're serious.

I've were given a incredible instance for you right here too. Now an amazing pal of mine installation a webpage whilst we had been in our early days at the scene. He had a quite proper product subsidized up via way of means of a multi stage associate gadget, or a matrix of sorts. Anyway, he began out selling and all become going well, till phrase began out spreading round a number of his associates approximately a few assured signups webpage that offered signups to something unfastened, for a charge.

Now unluckily I'm certain you may see what is coming. Not simplest did the associates pass for this one, which wasn't plenty assist to them, due to route maximum of those untargeted humans had been simply freebie seekers signing up due to the fact they had been getting something in go back from the assured signups sites, and simplest a tiny percent had been sincerely going for his web website hosting bundle or the pay plan he had in place. What he ended up with become a gadget clogged complete of humans that had no concept what they had been subscribing to, were not making him or themselves or the humans that referred them any money, and had no hobby in doing so. A real aid catastrophe case, that one, as it rendered the pay plan almost useless. Make certain you try this one proper and provide a tribulation for a small charge if your product permits. You can be searching at a comparable luxurious state of affairs otherwise.

Banning the Word Cheap

Rule seven: Never inform absolutely everyone your product is cheap. Yuck. Nothing foremost to stay on here, really, however by no means ever describe your merchandise as cheap. Competitively priced - yes, the fine rate for that service - yes, cheap - no manner. That simply devalues your product complete stop. More frequently than now no longer, human beings do not need cheap. They need first-rate at a terrific rate, specially in on-line business.

Rule eight: Don't be afraid to test with pricing strategies. I can understand the way you is probably involved that clients, who offered your product costing four hundred dollars, could be irritated that they get hold of an electronic mail for a special seasonal provide slicing that fee in half, however it significantly would not paintings that manner. You're now no longer offending absolutely everyone with the aid of using doing this, and it is the most effective manner you may come up with new strategies and strategies your self, via testing.

The truth is actual international organizations do that all of the time. They have extraordinary sales, then they positioned charges up at Christmas time and precise instances of the year while their merchandise are going to be extra in demand, cut price matters daily, upload and remove reductions and so on. It's now no longer a incorrect factor to do. It's now no longer unethical. It's business. And in case your clients have ever left their homes to head and buy something from a store, they will understand this too.

So here is the deal. If you want a few greater coins, why now no longer provide a restricted number of members, a protracted subscription at a reduction of a month or so during the year? I even have to mention this one works actual well, and I had a huge percent of my member base from my preceding webpage hand me huge up the front wads of coins that I ought to positioned to appropriate use making extra coins. If I'd left them at their twenty greenback per month fee, I would possibly have made a further few hundred dollars, however at a slower pace.

There's not anything incorrect with you including reductions to the quit of 5 or six day follow-up messages, so on and so forth. In truth, there is not anything incorrect with converting your rate in your major web page with none caution or notice. Don't fall into the lure of annoying what preceding clients are going to mention, due to the fact significantly, this occurs withinside the actual international all of the time. I understand in all my experimental days I've by no means had a person come to me and shout or complain due to the fact I pulled 1 / 4 off the rate an afternoon when they offered it. If you've got a first-rate product, that is appropriate enough, now no longer to say you owe it to your self to try specific strategies like withinside the above examples till you get matters lifeless perfect.

Value Added

Rule nine: Always upload fee. We've were given an entire phase that talks approximately adding fee in a moment, thru bonuses, one of a kind approaches, promo's, and the like. But for now, take into account while developing with a fee to your product, do not permit it be the simplest product. Strange sentence indeed, however have a take a observe it this way, what type of matters are going to can help you boom your fee and in fact convince humans to shop for your stuff on the equal time?

The great of your product and income gadget are the obvious, however how approximately bonuses? What approximately testimonials from acknowledged and depended on humans on your field? It's now no longer simply fabric matters either. What approximately your popularity and the way others see you? So here is a very last tidbit of recommendation for you. If you sense that your product isn't really well worth the 4 hundred bucks you are charging then boom its fee thru those methods. If you continue to do not sense it is really well worth it, then at this point, you realize that you are charging an excessive amount for it.

Ok, I'll be sincere with you. If you need to be successful and get your fee simply right, with out being 'cheap' you need to perform a little work. A little studies and a touch mind work. It's now no longer all simple one three. Understand that it is now no longer approximately being inexpensive than every person else, it is approximately pricing your product correctly relying on competition, who you are aiming your product at, its great, and your studies and monitoring results.

By now you need to have a clean concept how a great deal you need to charge, and the way you will cross approximately it. If you have, great. Just take into account, the fee you put up there on release day does not ought to be set in stone with the aid of using any means. It's there to be tinkered and performed with the aid of using you till you sense it is correct, and your testing indicates you that it's correct. Have a touch self belief on your stuff. Next time you create that top notch information product, club site, or piece of software, strive to keep away from promoting it at rock backside prices, due to the fact I guarantee you, it is now no longer gaining you income, it is dropping you them.

Summary

- In this segment I'd like to speak to you approximately pricing strategies, and display you the form of versatility we've got as on line entrepreneurs with our very own merchandise. Many appear to simply throw on a charge just like what they suppose their product is really well worth, or have a take a observe others and attempt to beat the opposition.

- Because our merchandise and the manner they may be offered is so extensive and varied, there's extra to pricing your product than meets the eye.

- A lot of humans question me why I cross into a lot element while speaking approximately fees amongst different subjects. They say get on with it, I simply need to make a few coins quickly. Well my solution to this is, if It's all properly and proper if a person tells you how some thing works, however if the state of affairs changes (which it regularly does in enterprise, and fast) you want to recognize the intricacies of why some thing labored in the primary place, permitting you to evolve your strategies to the converting situations while not having to shop for a manual whenever new tendencies appear.

- So, how can we determine upon our pricing? Does opposition rely and what need to I think about while pricing my product? Should I be less expensive? Should I be extra highly-priced? How do I recognize while to be which and why? Should I supply unique gives to unique corporations of humans? Who? Why? Should I provide unique variations of my product at unique fees? How do I do that, and the way do I recognize if I'm doing proper? A shed load of questions and solutions we're going to be covering on this segment.

- So right here's my pinnacle policies for a success pricing of any product which you create, and the questions which you need to be asking your self as you undergo this process, as constantly from the floor up.

- Rule one: Don't charge your self too low. A low charge does not imply extra profit. When you are looking at pricing, the primary component that could probable soar into your thoughts if I dispatched you off proper now to charge up your merchandise is what's the opposition charging? I'm going to price much less.

- Keep in thoughts from the start, your charge does not ought to in shape or beat every person else's, or maybe come near doing so to your merchandise to be a success.

- You do want to be privy to what others are charging for comparable merchandise, however that does not imply you want to conquer them. Why can not your product be the Mercedes or the Aston Martin of your preferred market? It's nonetheless a car, however it is the exceptional, a top rate product and the **charge displays** that.

- So, rule **quantity** one: If **you've got a top notch top rate** product, **do not** be afraid to bump the **charge** up. By **setting** your **charge** up and above the **opposition**, you are clearly **probably** to outsell **remarkable reasonably-priced opposition.** Why? Simple. Would you **anticipate** the **equal exceptional** from a $10 **route** as from a $1000 one? So there we have rule **quantity** . Never **charge your self** so low **which you suppose humans** will **appearance** and **suppose,** "Wow, that's a **exceptional** sounding product, **appearance** how little it costs!" Because **it's** now no longer what **they may be announcing** at all. They're **announcing,** "Wow, **have a take a observe** how little that costs. What's the catch?"

- In effect, all **you are doing right here is** including even **extra cost for your product** via a **better charge.** It is probably the **equal product,** however I'll let you know now, it is more likely to **promote** at a **charge** a person will **suppose** is reasonable, than some thing that knocks the reader off their chair at how reasonably-priced it is.

- Don't be a part of the crowds who're too afraid to even try and bump their fees up. Don't undervalue your self for the sake of being less expensive. If you've got a higher product, you cross in advance and positioned a better charge on it. People will quickly pay attention approximately the way you're really well worth each penny.

- I may want to display you such a lot of merchandise which might be accessible proper now, in opposition with every different, however one is charging a heck of lots extra than the different. How approximately this manual as one? Here we're charging you one thousand bucks for the complete set of manuals, however there are lots of different courses accessible that fee ten bucks. Will the exceptional of each of them be the equal? Looking on the charge alone, from a customer's factor of view, I noticeably doubt it.

- How approximately the trendy buy you made to your house, whether or not it became a entire paintings surface, a toaster, a dinner table, some thing it became. If you observed back, a while in the past matters have been the opposite. People desired matters that have been properly priced, reasonably-priced, and that they labored. They have been realistic and affordable. Times have changed.

- Nowadays, it is were given to be the fastest, the exceptional, the maximum powerful, the nicest, the simplest and least trouble to use. Now is the exceptional time to capitalize on this. Don't positioned your merchandise withinside the good buy bin if they may be top rate merchandise. More on this later.

- Next up, provide alternatives to your clients. A Pro and a Lite model for instance. Not every person can manage to pay for a top rate product, and a lite model is simply the ticket.

- On **pinnacle** of this, taking the above reason, **now no longer every person** can **manage to pay for top rate merchandise**, so **provide** up a choice. Selling **top rate merchandise is all properly** and **proper**, however while the **charge begins off evolved** to get a **touch better**, you **want** to cater to **folks who can not purchase in a single cross** as they'll do with **much less highly-priced merchandise**.

- Next up, **praise schemes**. It's **now no longer tough** to provide you with approaches to **praise** them. Right now, I'm **setting collectively** an ID **quantity gadget** for myself that allows **preceding clients** to return back alongside and **purchase my stuff at a reduced rate**.

- These **humans** are the **maximum vital** of all. You've already **were given** them on your lists, **they have got already offered your stuff,** this means that they may be inclined to spend money, and of **route** they **believe you,** and **they may be extreme approximately** looking extra information, or the goods and offerings you provide. Remember this, due to the fact if you neglect about you will cross broke. It's as easy as that. You need to preserve the clients which might be shopping for from you happy, and also you need to live in contact with them. If you do not exit of your manner to delight them, you will ought to exit and spend wads extra on getting new clients. Look after them, due to the fact they will be with you for a long term to return back and could shape the bottom of a success enterprise from the phrase cross.

- Rule six: Avoid unfastened trials. Trial intervals are regularly a popular characteristic for a club webpage, however except you need to waste some time and assets on freebie seekers, installation a limited, much less highly-priced trial for them. A greenback for the first month for instance, in any other case you may locate your self questioning why your clients are not shopping for something extra from you. It's probably due to the fact they didn't need to shop for withinside the first place, a waste of some time.

- I've were given a top notch instance for you right here too. Now a very good pal of mine installation a webpage while we have been in our early days at the scene. He had a quite proper product subsidized up through a multi degree associate gadget, or a matrix of sorts. Anyway, he commenced selling and all became going properly, till phrase commenced spreading around a number of his associates approximately a few assured signups webpage that offered signups to something unfastened, for a charge.

- Now, unfortunately, I'm certain you may see what is coming. Not most effective did the associates cross for this one, which wasn't a whole lot assist to them, due to route maximum of those untargeted humans have been simply freebie seekers signing up due to the fact they have been getting some thing in go back from the assured signups sites, and most effective a tiny percent have been clearly going for his web website hosting package deal or the pay plan he had in place. What he ended up with became a gadget clogged complete of humans that had no concept what they have been subscribing to, were not making him or themselves or the humans that referred them any money, and had no hobby in doing so. A actual aid disaster, that one. Make certain you do that one proper and provide a tribulation for a small charge in case your product permits. You may be searching at a comparable high priced state of affairs in any other case.

- Rule quantity seven. Never say your product is reasonably-priced. It's fee effective, a very good deal, however in no way reasonably-priced, which indicates a loss of exceptional.

- Rule eight. Don't be afraid to test with pricing strategies. I can apprehend the way you is probably involved that clients that offered your product costing 4 hundred bucks could be aggravated that they acquire an email for a unique seasonal provide slicing that fee in half, however it critically does not paintings that manner. You're now no longer offending everyone through doing this, and it is the most effective manner you will come up with new strategies and processes your self, via testing.

- The truth is, actual international companies do that all of the time. They have remarkable income, positioned fees up at Christmas time and unique instances of the 12 months while their merchandise are going to be extra in demand, bargain matters daily, upload and remove reductions and so on. It's now no longer a incorrect component to do, it is now no longer unethical, it is enterprise. And in case your clients have ever left their homes to move and buy some thing from a store, they will recognize this.

- So, right here's the deal. If you want a few greater coins, why now no longer provide a limited quantity of participants an extended subscription at a reduction of a month or so during the 12 months? I actually have to mention this one works actual properly, and I had a big percent of my member base from my preceding webpage hand me big up front wads of coins that I may want to positioned to proper use making extra coins. If I'd left them at their twenty greenback according to month charge, I may have made an additional few hundred bucks, however at a slower pace.

- Rule nine. We've were given an entire segment that talks approximately including cost later on, via bonuses, unique approaches, promotions, and the like. But for now, recollect while arising with a charge to your product, do not allow your product be the most effective product. Strange sentence indeed, however have a take a observe it this manner, what form of matters are going to can help you boom your charge and in fact convince humans to shop for your stuff?

- The exceptional of your product and income gadget are the obvious, however how approximately bonuses? What approximately testimonials from recognized and depended on humans for your field? It's now no longer simply cloth matters either. What approximately your recognition and the way others understand you? So here is a very last tidbit of recommendation for you. If you experience that your product is not really well worth the 4 hundred bucks you are charging then boom its cost via those strategies. If you continue to do not experience it is really well worth it, then at this factor, you already know which you're charging an excessive amount of for it, and your monitoring records will let you know that also.

- Ok, I'll be sincere with you. If you need to prevail and get your charge simply proper, with out being 'reasonably-priced' you need to perform a little paintings. A little studies and a touch mind paintings. It's now no longer all clear-cut one three. Understand that it is now no longer approximately being less expensive than everyone else, it is approximately pricing your product correctly relying on opposition, who you are aiming your product at, its exceptional, and your ongoing monitoring and testing.

- By now, you need to have a clean concept how a whole lot

you need to price, and the way you'll cross approximately it. If you've got got, top notch. Just recollect, the charge you positioned up there on release day does not ought to be set in stone through any means. It's there to be tinkered and performed with through you till you experience it is correct. Have a touch self belief for your stuff. Next time you create that high-quality data product, club webpage, or piece of software, attempt to keep away from promoting it at rock backside fees, due to the fact I guarantee you, it is now no longer gaining you income, it is dropping you them.

2. *Overview of Added Value*

- To introduce **standards** of including fee earlier than and after the sale of your product, **preserving** your **clients** happy, and **setting** extra cash to your pocket.

- To **display** you the way to begin searching round you, and to **begin** seeing what other **human beings** are doing with their **fee** including, mainly the successful.

- To **communicate** approximately testimonials and **the way to** take them **in addition** to **encourage** solid **self belief** in **your self** from the **clients** perspective.

- To **appearance carefully** at **widespread** bonuses, and to keep away from a number of the pitfalls of other entrepreneurs now no longer in know, who **smash** their income with the aid of using looking to upload fee incorrectly.

- To provide you with 3 actual lifestyles examples of actual entrepreneurs which have attempted to upload fee, however executed so incorrectly in a single manner or another, and to reveal you the way to keep away from devastating your income with the aid of using doing the same.

- To display that worthwhile loyalty is going a protracted manner to growing income, and now and again generating a couple of income from a unmarried product, meaning double the income to your pocket.

- To exhibit how a easy method will make certain that your clients take into account you and your product for a long term to come, main to in addition income down the line, and best bulge to your pocket.

Adding Value Explained

Welcome to the including cost in your merchandise phase. You might also additionally don't forget we talked a touch approximately this in advance withinside the income letter writing sections, however we didn't pretty move into the intensity that I might have liked, so I stored it for right here instead.

In this phase we're going to be speaking approximately a way to immediately affect your income via the addition of cost on your merchandise, starting from offers, joint mission deals, session fees, bonuses and others. You see, it is all approximately perceived cost, and getting the maximum from your product. Again, some thing we mentioned in pricing strategies, became getting the rate you watched your product merits and persuading humans to shop for it via way of means of stacking on motives for them to do so, some thing as soon as mastered, will push humans over the threshold once more and once more, pushing them over the threshold via way of means of hitting the purchase button to your site.

Most importantly of all, there is a whole lot of approaches of pulling this off, and they may be forever changing, and entrepreneurs are developing with increasingly more modern approaches to upload cost to their merchandise. It's really well worth looking in fact, subsequent time you locate yourself studying via a income letter or a few advert copy, examine how they upload cost to their provide the usage of matters that are not immediately associated with the product itself. Watching how others do matters on their websites is one of the maximum precious price unfastened and quite an awful lot attempt unfastened manner of doing matters you've got to your arsenal, however it works extraordinarily well. Keep that during thoughts all of the time, now no longer simply in the course of this phase.

Come returned right here as soon as you've got were given your product up and strolling if you're now no longer operating on that proper now, due to the fact all of those are factors of a income letter in a few manner or another, bar two. So we could get started. How approximately taking it from the pinnacle and beginning with the maximum used and widely recognized and operating right all the way down to the least broadly used, and the brand new and modern ideas.

Cut Off Dates

Cut off dates and **restrained** numbers: A **splendid vicinity to begin** and **definitely smooth** to slip into any **income** letter for any product. The **antique reduce** off dates are **probable** the most **broadly** used out of all **of those** methods, **and that they appear** to **nonetheless** be working. All this **calls for is** notification of your low **charge most effective being assured** till a selected date. These are **splendid phrases** to use, **due to the fact in case you** do determine to increase the deadline, you **may locate** that you could with out inflicting a stir. Way too frequently recently I've visited **websites** that say the **charge** may be going up for **positive** on a selected date, however it **in no way** does, and the date magically **actions ahead every day.** Not a good **manner** to be doing **commercial enterprise I can guarantee** you.

This is catering extra to the impulse customers in place of including value, however I idea we might get that during there too anyway, as it is really well worth a point out for positive.

Limited Numbers Done Right

Next up is the **restrained numbers** technique: Only permitting a restrained wide variety of **human beings** into the **webpage** at a specific **time**, or **handiest** permitting a specific quantity of human beings to **purchase** at a specific price. Again, pretty extensively used, and **each** catering to impulse **consumers** in addition to including value, relying on which **technique you are** using. Now this one I **specifically** like. One of my **preceding websites** has this very **device** up and running, **in which** I handiest allow some hundred **participants** in at a time. It's a membership **webpage** of course, so re-**going on earning** all **round** for me, and it makes my **participants sense a bit** lucky. Some of them have even **instructed** me this themselves, and I've had requests from my **listing** on **numerous events** asking while a gap **will** turn out to be to be had due to the fact they genuinely desired to get in.

Now you may say that I'm dropping cash on this kind of deal, handiest letting human beings in a small wide variety at a time, however it genuinely would not manifest like that. The cause the limit became set withinside the first area became in order that I'd have time to begin running on different tasks and will run my different websites on autopilot, so that you should say I discovered this one with the aid of using accident. Don't overlook that you could usually improve and decrease your limits in case you do strive this, which I exceedingly propose you do strive, although proscribing numbers doesn't match your situation, proscribing numbers on a decrease price, very probably will match each situation, now no longer to say it usually amazes me how some distance phrase of mouth travels approximately this.

Standard Testimonials

Next up is the highly sizable and famous preferred testimonial. I'm only going to the touch on this, due to the fact there genuinely is not a massive quantity to say, and I tremendously doubt every person available has by no means visible one. A preferred phase of text both at some point of your income letter, down the aspect of your nav bar, on a separate web page or a database of satisfied clients works without a hassle and is going a lengthy manner to cementing to your clients minds that your product is good. This is in particular genuine if the individual or humans writing are widely recognized and revered in your field. Try to get in touch with as a minimum one well-known, hand them your product for free, and request a testimonial for it.

Testimonials - But Better

Now, let's examine the marginally rarer audio testimonials. These cement fee in your product even in addition and growth patron self belief no end. I've in my opinion checked out textual content testimonials before, and visible a few predominant flaws that gave away to me, and proved virtually that they had been faked. This pretty a great deal placed a massive dent in what I idea of this stuff early on, and I've even had human beings come to me and inform me they faked their testimonials withinside the past. Needless to mention I wasn't satisfied approximately that. Granted, audio testimonials may be faked too, however it is commonly now no longer some thing that pops into your head while listening in comparison to studying written ones, as a result the massive self belief booster and fee including of this method.

If you could get a few audio testimonials, whether or not you ask human beings to name your answering gadget and feature them depart messages, or in case you are capable of record over the internet via voice communications, it is nicely really well worth it. The more effort is available in and hits your clients with a huge improve to self belief resulting in the long run in extra income and assets for you and your business. Can't be bad.

The Ultimate Testimonial

Ok, seeing as we have got completed the audio and textual content issue with those testimonials, shall we go all out, most important bells and whistles professionalism with video testimonials. How regularly do you notice streaming video testimonials up on websites? Not very regularly I'd say. In reality on the time of writing this, I've most effective visible in my entire career, and they had been great. Real human beings giving actual debts of the use of actual merchandise that worked. If any kind of testimonial goes to feature cost in your merchandise, it is going to be this one. A easy concept advanced into an all making a song all dancing, hard hitting approach that works.

The subsequent excellent issue to video testimonials might be inviting those human beings over to your own home to inform you the way right the goods are. I admit, that is taking matters to an extreme, however with all of the virtual cameras floating round nowadays, and the capacity to seize video via the net, and the bigger website hosting areas beginning to seem via the concept competition, it should not be extra than a bit time ingesting to get some of those. Well really well worth it in my opinion. Taking testimonials to the max.

The Standard Bonus

Right, I assume we have got executed approximately as an awful lot as we are able to with the ones testimonials, so shifting on a bit to bonuses. Standard bonuses. Nothing fancy genuinely, all you're doing is providing up a few kind of bonus with the acquisition of the product, again including cost. Generally those are referred to as some thing at once associated with your product, or maybe better, some thing with the intention to gain you in addition to the patron getting it for free.

How approximately placing collectively a small schooling collection that lets in the patron to provide it away, constructing your reputation, in addition to including cost at the preliminary sale? Or if you are genuinely on a brainy one which day, how approximately placing some thing collectively with the intention to make you cash thru teaching the buyer? For example, provide away an associate advertising and marketing path on your customers, supporting them grow to be better affiliates, letting them sell your stuff and make you cash on the same time.

Bonuses - But Smarter

It's hyperlinks like this that make up truly smart bonuses, in which at the floor they would possibly simply appear well known to different human beings that do not recognize in which you're coming from. Always attempt to positioned some thing collectively in order to gain you as nicely as the customer, whether or not it is elevated sales, a re-branded book packed with associate hyperlinks or hyperlinks for your product they could supply away, or an academic tool in order to help your customer, and positioned cash to your pocket on the identical time.

In fact, whilst we are speaking approximately gifting away bonuses to decorate your product, I've even visible a few truly powerful merchandise which might be simply made from a group of bonuses, without a actual principal product. Of route they have got a principal theme, and are all associated in a few way, however that is some thing to preserve in thoughts for whilst you've been going some time and having a gradual day. As lengthy as all of the merchandise praise every different, and are relevant, they could come collectively to make a complete new product and profits circulate for yourself.

Bonuses Done Right

While we are in this subject, please, please take observe right here, due to the fact if I see all and sundry looking to flog their product, questioning that an book entitled ' Doing enterprise these days, withinside the 60's' goes to shift greater in their merchandise, I definitely would possibly need to begin questioning approximately peoples motives. Things like this might not upload $500 to your charge. In fact, permit me let you know how extreme this difficulty is. If you positioned a dodgy bonus together, or do that withinside the incorrect manner, you may devalue your product so an awful lot, that it will become worthless, and also you simply might not promote any. Simple as that.

So here is a widespread rule for you. If you've got definitely concept approximately it, dug approximately and attempted to locate some thing to feature in as a terrific profitable bonus to try to tip clients over the brink and to have greater of them purchase your product, and also you actually can not locate some thing that suits the bill, go together with not anything or create an original data product your self. No bonuses are higher than one which places all your clients off. As apparent as that sounds, it appears to be going on greater and greater regularly recently, that is extraordinary, due to the sheer variety of human beings that declare to understand what they are speaking approximately which can be coaching human beings what to do with on-line enterprise nowadays.

Using the instance above I need to illustrate some thing to you presently that also appears to have emerge as a extraordinary epidemic that quite an awful lot makes me and all and sundry else I understand click on proper off the internet site and cross someplace else whilst searching out their merchandise, and that is whilst human beings take an excessive amount of time and installed a little an excessive amount of attempt into including price to one in every of their merchandise. Or so that they suppose anyway. Have a examine this one, how normally have you ever visible this recently?

Example: Get your difficult hitting, extensive schooling direction, entitled 'Improve Your Fishing', such as CD's filled with audio and video, displaying you all the tricks, suggestions and procedures in use these days through a number of the maximum a success fisherman in the world!. Order now and get this tested direction really well worth over $2500 for a measly $300. In fact, I'm so assured that it is going that will help you I'm going to knock the charge down in addition. You can get all this information in a single area for an amazing $49.95. Order your replica now!

See in which I'm coming from? Don't get me incorrect, there may be not anything incorrect with giving unique gives to folks who purchase there after which catering to impulse buyers, and good buy hunters, or simply to expose human beings they are getting a actual desirable deal out of you, however from

$2500 right all the way down to $49.95? That's going over the pinnacle, and regrettably simply makes your product appear to be a defect. How could you experience if you walked into a shop and noticed a pinnacle of the variety 85" display screen TV knocked down from $3000 to $200? I can let you know, your first response could both be 'Yeah proper, that is a joke', or maybe greater likely 'What's the catch?' or 'What's incorrect with it?'.

Remember whilst we talked in advance approximately growing consumer self assurance to your merchandise, and the entire concept of a income letter is to squish most of these troubles and questions human beings would possibly have with a product, whilst on the equal time developing a need, and occasionally even a want for it. Do you notice how including an excessive amount of price, too soon, or going definitely over the pinnacle may be detrimental? Where as you notice it as giving the clients a good buy, they are seeing it as some other query in their minds. Another hurdle that they want to cross, or a query they want to locate the solution to earlier than they purchase your product. It's anywhere nowadays. Discounts are not horrific on their own, however on this sort of circumstance, they may be going to kill your income. Most human beings do not even understand why. If you failed to earlier than, now you do. Don't make the identical mistake.

Now one factor I do not need to do is will let you suppose that there's most effective one horrific manner to upload price (or absolutely take away price) out of your merchandise, due to the fact I've visible it accomplished time and again once more in special circumstances. I turned into going to present you 3 examples right here, however shall we take the fishing instance above as one, and I'm going to present you greater, in absolutely special conditions in an effort to smash your income figures. Bear in thoughts those are actual, stay examples which can be accessible proper now on the internet.

Example one: The 'Only need your bonuses' factor: I land in

this quite blue and white, professionally designed, nicely constructed internet site that right away makes me smile (Just feels high-quality whilst some thing is provided like this). I continue to examine the income replica which in short tells me how I can get cash-making suggestions free of charge if I join up to their publication. I see hyperlinks to returned problems right here too so I'm now no longer definitely positioned off through the mind of this being some other terrible excuse to ship me ads. Then comes the standard, join up these days and get this freebie. I'm happy, as it appears applicable to what I need to achieve. Now typically at this factor I'd simply cross and join up, however this man or woman determined to head the greater manner to delight me.

Book 1, Book 2, Book 3, Book 4, Software 1, Software 2, Software 3, Software 4,5,6,7 and so forth. Now at the floor this could appear to be including price to the factor of human beings now no longer being capable of refuse, however actually, are human beings signing as much as their loose publication for the freebies or for the content material? Again, at first look getting greater subscribers is right proper? Well, now no longer definitely. Not if none of them care approximately your content material and simply desired your series of 50 thousand books. Remember, it is all approximately fine, now no longer quantity, and this situation shows precisely how you may upload an excessive amount of price to a loose a product for your detriment in the end. Your fine suffers, so does your pocket, and you have got absolutely wasted your time.

Example : The 'Not positive what going on' factor: Here's a terrific one which I see a lot of, and some thing else that's at the upward push too. In fact, to be honest, I definitely suppose this one is our fault, it is us promoting those publications that let you know to promote your bonuses like they are merchandise themselves. This is accurate information, however it is able to be taken too some distance.

Again, I'm browsing across the internet and land on a domain that takes place to be a cash making op. I'm now no longer against cash making possibilities of direction, and this one simply takes place to have a splendid headline that entices me to examine in addition. The in addition I get down the income letter the higher it gets, till we hit the bonuses. Book one, click on right here to examine approximately this book (forwards me to an entire new income letter), click on right here to examine approximately this software (takes me to an entire new income letter) and so forth for 3 or 4 bonuses. By the time I'm accomplished, I've been taken all around the area, have 5 home windows open, examine six income letters which every try to promote me directly to some thing else, and feature hassle locating my manner returned for your income letter.

It's critical to consider to feature price the use of bonuses in a manner which makes your bonuses appear to be actual merchandise themselves, however by no means ever lose sight of what you need your internet site to do. Don't throw human beings off in special directions and feature them examine ten income letters for special merchandise. It simply would not work like that. Again whilst you might imagine you are including price, all you are doing is distracting and puzzling your visitors. When human beings say promote your bonuses like a actual product, they imply some difficult hitting paragraphs approximately how this compliments the primary product and you are getting a heck of a terrific deal, or you can not get it everywhere else, or in which it is been tested etc. Don't cross over the pinnacle, or once more, you will be dropping clients.

Just those above examples (3 in case you encompass the fishing one) I see each unmarried day, and the worst factor approximately it is, whilst human beings say to me, 'Why no income from my site?' and I inform them that components in their bonuses sections are destroying their income letter, I get extraordinary appears and comments. See it is like one in every of the ones little disturbing thoughts puzzles, in which the answer is so apparent human beings pass over it, and I can inform they do not experience too proud approximately that, however no worries. Not a hassle at all, so long as you analyze from it and do not repeat the error you may do satisfactory I inform them.

Now in case you've examine this some distance and are in the end stressed or misplaced as to what the heck you can probable provide as an advantage similarly for your product, or do not have some thing to hand, do not worry. It would not need to be tangible at all. It would not have to be an vintage ebook (in fact, it might in all likelihood be useful if it wasn't an vintage ebook) it would not need to be a bit of software. Open your thoughts a touch and suppose approximately different matters you can provide to human beings in conjunction with your product. Are you respected to your discipline of information? How approximately a loose one hour, no strings smartphone or video session together along with your consumer's purchase, or maybe a follow-up session to see how they've **accomplished** with the product you've **simply offered** them?

This **isn't always any such difficult factor** to put into effect when **you have** the knowledge. Personally, I like my **loose** time, and also you might not get me **speaking** to you at the smartphone approximately your enterprise until you've got simply deposited $500 into my account for the hour, and heck, you'll need to understand me quite nicely and be in my desirable books to get me right all the way down to that charge too. Immediately that **provides price** to this product with out me even providing the consultations, due to the fact I can inform you presently, it took a touch longer than 3 hours to jot down this guide. This is some thing you may do too, and in case you definitely desired there may be not anything incorrect with going a step in addition and in reality providing the ones consultations, perhaps half-hour or an hour according to consumer loose (depending of direction on what number of clients you intend to get according to week. Be cautious now no longer to try to present a hundred human beings a loose 3 hour session each week).

You do not need to be withinside the enterprise of promoting publications and data approximately enterprise to positioned any of this together. It would not count what you are promoting, you may use this approach somewhere, whether or not it is an hour loose technical support, or a loose 30 minute self assurance builder to praise your foremost product. It's absolutely as much as you. Be imaginative, and hey, it would even result in in addition consultations placing even greater coins to your pocket. Again, a freebie enables your clients and also you, now no longer simply your clients. An critical factor, indeed, and a query you must be asking your self whilst developing any price including material. How does this assist my clients and me?

A Little Something Extra

Before we flow on, there may be extra approaches I'd like to speak to you approximately including cost to a product. This time, though, the bonuses we will be imparting are not directly associated with the product, and are not always given at the income letter as maximum bonuses are. It's usually pleasant to present the patron a touch some thing greater, and that is one manner to do this and once more, as we pointed out earlier than, assisting yourself in addition to the patron.

The first instance I need to speak approximately is including an alternative for reductions associated with your different merchandise, both now, or withinside the destiny thru a price price tag system. A good manner to do that is permit clients to feature extra merchandise to their purchasing cart at a reduced charge after they take a look at out. Not simplest does it permit them some thing greater for a touch less, however it permits you to make extra income on the identical time, once more, reaping benefits each you and your patron.

If that is the primary product you are creating, it would not harm to praise loyalty. How approximately giving them 10% off the following product they purchase out of your enterprise? This won't appear like it's going to do an awful lot at the surface, however whilst you switch a primary time patron right into a long time patron that continues shopping for from you once more and once more, that is including cost on your merchandise at it is finest, as it advantages you the maximum now no longer simply today, however a ways into the destiny, wherein your preceding clients are choosing up , three, four, or even extra of your merchandise inside a year.

And last, some thing it truly is alternatively underestimated and not often used (at least thru the goods I've bought through the years anyway) is once more, approximately profitable loyalty. If for a few cause you do not need to consist of unique bonuses at the income letter, why now no longer move for some thing a touch exclusive as an alternative, and hit them with it when they purchase the product. Granted, you are dropping your extra income strength thru imparting this to your income letter, and as an alternative handing it out after the sale, however permit me guarantee you, in case you do this, you may be remembered, and most significantly humans will speak approximately you, and on the identical time become long time, dependable clients of yours. Is there some thing extra valuable?

Above all, in case you take not anything else far from this, I need you to don't forget one thing, and that is that not anything in enterprise is ready in stone. No policies that exist now will exist forever, not anything that works now will paintings forever. The identical applies to the whole lot written earlier than you. Experiment, innovate, be exclusive and you may be remembered, make wads of coins and get your call around, and who knows, in six months time **you would possibly simply** be sitting **wherein** I am now, typing out a report revealing the **most modern and maximum slicing area advertising techniques** that you've that you've got determined in the course of your journey.

SUMMARY

- In this phase we will be taking the idea of including cost similarly, while we look at without delay influencing your income thru the addition of cost, ranging from particularly crafted offers, JV deals, consultations, bonuses and others to reveal perceived cost or intangible items is as suitable as financial cost with tangible items.

- There are many approaches to feature cost in your product, and the manner and strategies are for all time converting thru new and modern twists on current techniques. It's really well worth searching out for those the subsequent time you examine a powerful income letter from a relied on marketer, and asking yourself, how are they including cost to their merchandise? Watching how others do matters on their websites is one of the maximum precious value unfastened and quite a good deal attempt unfastened manner of studies that you have on your arsenal, however it really works extraordinarily well. Keep that during thoughts all of the time, now no longer simply at some stage in this phase.

- A suitable area to begin right here is reduce off dates and confined numbers in your income letters. Probably the maximum used and widely recognized other than testimonials, this one in reality receives the income flowing if carried out correctly.

- All the reduce off dates require is notification that a unique provide is finishing on a specific day, giving the impact that the reader will leave out in the event that they do not purchase now, an age-vintage and well-used, however powerful, manner of pushing domestic extra income.

- If the usage of this technique, use the language that indicates that your low rate and your unique provide is simplest assured till a selected date, this manner if you make a decision to retain to a later date it would not reason a stir, and you may keep away from the usage of the ones little java codes that push the date forwards every day regarding the laptop clock time on the traffic end.

• Second, reflect on confined numbers, simplest permitting a confined variety of human beings into your website online a selected factor in time. Again, pretty broadly used, and both catering to impulse buys and including cost. One of my preceding websites has this device set up, and nevertheless to this day, I actually have human beings asking if there may be a area open yet, or even presenting extra money than he popular rate to get in.

• Now you would possibly say that I'm dropping cash on the sort of deal, simplest letting human beings in a small variety at a time, however it in reality would not manifest like that. The purpose the restrict become set withinside the first area become in order that I'd have time to begin operating on different tasks and will run my different websites on autopilot, so that you should say I discovered this one with the aid of using accident. Don't neglect about that you may usually boost and decrease your limits in case you do strive this, which I fairly propose you do strive, although proscribing numbers doesn't fit your situation, proscribing numbers on a decrease rate, very in all likelihood will fit each situation.

- The subsequent technique of including cost is the testimonial. Again, we have got mentioned this previously, however it merits a mention. A popular bite of textual content both well placed for your income letter, or down the aspect for your nav bar, or maybe a entire phase committed to client remarks and testimonials. This does wonders for evidence of your merchandise capabilities and including cost.

- Taking testimonials to the subsequent step: How approximately pulling in audio? Simply setting up your answering device to record, and letting your clients understand it is there for them to depart audio testimonials is a excellent manner to feature realism and a piece of believability in your client remarks, what's greater, they are now no longer precisely clean to fake, so that you're inducing even greater believe together along with your readers.

• How approximately taking matters even similarly with video testimonials? I noticed a specific marketer doing this only a few months returned, and it made his income letter in reality sticky, memorable and powerful. Considering I neglect about approximately income letters simply a few hours later except I analyze some thing, or they are quite unique and unique, this is some thing I urge you to strive when you have the equipment to position this collectively.

• Next up, popular bonuses. Again, allow no longer reside at the fundamentals of this because we have got already mentioned them, however how approximately taking popular bonus giveaways a touch similarly?

- How approximately placing collectively a small education collection that permits the client to provide it away constructing your reputation, in addition to including cost at the preliminary sale? Or, in case you're in reality on a brainy one which day, how approximately placing some thing collectively so as to make you cash thru instructing the buyer. For example, gifting away an associate advertising direction in your clients supporting them emerge as higher affiliates, and with a bit of luck sell your stuff and make you cash on the equal time.

- It's hyperlinks like this that make up in reality smart bonuses, wherein at the floor they may simply appear popular to different human beings that do not apprehend wherein you are coming from. Always attempt to placed some thing collectively so as to gain you in addition to the client, whether or not it is multiplied income, a re-branded product packed with associate hyperlinks or hyperlinks in your product they could provide away, or an academic tool so as to help your client, and placed cash on your pocket on the equal time.

- In fact, even as we are speaking approximately about gifting away bonuses to decorate your product, I've even visible a few in reality powerful merchandise which are simply made from a gaggle of bonuses, and not using a actual relevant factor of focus. Of direction they've a relevant theme, and are all associated in a few manner, however that is some thing to maintain in thoughts for while you've got been going some time and are having a sluggish day or need to prepare a function packed club web website online. As lengthy as all the goods praise every different, and are relevant, they could come collectively to make an entire new product and earnings circulate for yourself.

- My subsequent factor is: Don't upload cost to the factor of taking it away. Imagine if I attempted to provide you an advantage with this direction and instructed you it become called 'Business in cutting-edge day 60's' after which went beforehand and instructed you it is really well worth $500, as an vintage maybe, however not anything greater.

• If you've got in reality notion approximately it, dug approximately and attempted to locate some thing to feature in as an awesome profitable bonus to try to tip clients over the threshold and to have greater of them purchase your product, and also you truely cannot locate whatever that suits the bill, go along with not anything. No bonuses are higher than one which places all of your clients off. As apparent as that sounds, it appears to be happening an increasing number of often recently, that is strange, due to the sheer variety of human beings that declare to understand what they are speaking approximately which are coaching human beings what to do with online enterprise nowadays.

• Next is your rate. Have you ever visible the ones

merchandise that let you know that their product is really well worth 5 hundred dollars, after which crossed out subsequent to it's far a new rate with the authentic crossed out of $250, then that rate is crossed out and subsequent to it's far a $20 rate tag? I suppose human beings are smarter than quite a few income letters provide them credit score for.

- There's not anything incorrect with giving those forms of alerts out to human beings, however $500 to $20? I do not suppose so. The response is both 'yeah right, that is a joke', or greater in all likelihood, what the catch?, or 'OK what's incorrect with it?' surely devaluing to the factor of setting doubt withinside the clients thoughts once more.

- See how including an excessive amount of cost too soon, or going in reality over the pinnacle can be detrimental? Where you spot it as giving the client a bargain, they are seeing it as some other query of their minds. Another hurdle that they want to cross, or a query they want to locate the solution to earlier than they purchase your product. It's anywhere nowadays. Discounts are not horrific on their own, however on this kind of circumstance, they're going to kill your income. Most human beings do not even understand why. If you failed to earlier than, now you do. Don't make the equal mistake.

- Here are 3 actual-lifestyles examples that I've visible of human beings gifting away an excessive amount of cost to their detriment. Number one: I land in this quite blue and white professionally designed web website online, which at once makes me smile. I continue to examine the income copy, and I'm thrilled to document that the unfastened guide sounds potent enticing. I'm equipped to signal up, however earlier than I do, this character makes a decision to move out in their manner to lure me.

- Book bonus 1, 2, 3, 4, 5, 6, 7, 8, 9, 10, further to a 40 book library, software program 1, software program 2, software program 3, software program 4, software program 5. By the time I were given carried out studying approximately every one, I'd forgotten what the authentic product become. On the floor it is able to look like including cost, however are human beings signing up for his or her unfastened publication or the bonuses?

- Giving the earth away is a superb technique to get numbers, now no longer quality.

- Example two: right here's an awesome one which I see a lot, and some thing you've got in all likelihood visible earlier than, too. In fact, to be sincere I in reality suppose this one is our fault, it is us promoting those publications that let you know to promote your bonuses like they are merchandise themselves. This is accurate information, however it may be taken too far.

- Again, I'm browsing across the internet and land on a website that takes place to be a cash making op. I'm now no longer against cash making possibilities of direction, and this one simply takes place to have a excellent headline that entices me to examine similarly. The similarly I get down the income letter the higher it receives, till we hit the bonuses. Book one, click on right here to examine approximately this book (forwards me to an entire new income letter), click on right here to examine approximately this software program (takes me to a entire new income letter) and so forth for 3 or 4 bonuses. By the time I'm carried out, I've been taken everywhere in the area, have 5 home windows open and feature trouble locating my manner returned to the authentic income letter.

• It's essential to take into account to feature cost the usage of bonuses in a manner which makes your bonuses look like actual merchandise themselves, however in no way ever lose sight of what you need your internet site to do. Don't throw human beings off in exclusive directions and feature them examine ten income letters for exclusive merchandise.

- Two extra approaches of including cost: Number one, giving reductions for different merchandise on the checkout. Add this in your cart, and purchase them collectively and save 50%, an superb and speedy manner of creating double income in lots of situations. More coins for you, greater cost for the client. Of direction now no longer every person will take up your provide, however the few more income certain upload up.

- If that is the primary product you are creating, it would not harm to praise loyalty. How approximately giving them 10% off the subsequent product they purchase out of your enterprise? This may not look like it will do a good deal at the floor, however while you switch a primary time client right into a long time client that maintains shopping for from you once more and once more, that is including cost in your merchandise at its finest, as it blessings you longer term.

- Last, some thing it is instead underestimated and not often used (at least thru the goods I've bought through the years anyway) is once more, approximately profitable loyalty. If for a few purpose you do not need to encompass specific bonuses at the income letter, why now no longer move for some thing a touch exclusive alternatively, and hit them with it when they purchase the product? Granted, you are dropping your extra income electricity thru supplying this for your income letter, and alternatively handing it out after the sale, however allow me guarantee you, in case you do this, you'll be remembered, and most significantly human beings will speak approximately you, and on the equal time emerge as lengthy term, dependable clients of yours. Very precious.

- Above all, in case you take not anything else far from this phase of the guide, I need you to take into account one thing, and that is that not anything in enterprise is ready in stone. No regulations that exist now will exist for all time, not anything that works now will paintings for all time. The equal applies to the whole thing written earlier than you. Experiment, innovate, be exclusive and you'll be remembered, make wads of coins and get your name around, and who knows, in six months time you would possibly simply be sitting wherein I am now, typing out a document like this revealing the most modern advertising strategies that you've got discovered.

ABOUT THE AUTHOR

KANHA GUPTA is a professional Indian writer, business coach, web and graphic designer. He is a great digital artist. He is extremely fond of anything that is related to writing, digital design and all the yumminess attached to it. He's been freelancing for many years and focuses on writing and blog design for small businesses and online publishers. He always aims to reach his creative goals one step at a time and believes in doing everything with a smile.

SOME IMPORTANT DIGITAL PRODUCTS

1) Natural Solutions For High Blood Pressure :-

https://291c9gfmwyh09td9p6n-vt2p63.hop.clickbank.net/

2) The Natural Way to Supercharge and Maintain A Healthy Brain & Vision :-

https://13c6f9dlszjxfl7olqplme0i1d.hop.clickbank.net/

3) 100 FITNESS AND HEALTH E-BOOKS :-

https://57c1d9eipyfy9z36kj27v9ry3w.hop.clickbank.net/

4) How I overcame anxiety disorder and started living life again :-

https://a176cjqdo2awfzc8xrwz5kgx0r.hop.clickbank.net/

5) Neuropathy No More :-

https://426ad9ccvzbshm4ps8zp2oieo7.hop.clickbank.net/

(Copy and Paste these links in any browser to avail them.)

THANK YOU FOR READING

THIS BOOK.

I HOPE YOU LIKE THIS.

www.ingramcontent.com/pod-product-compliance
Lightning Source LLC
Chambersburg PA
CBHW070630220526
45466CB00001B/142